Are we

LUCKY

or

WHAT

?

培育哈佛孩子

Andrew S.S. Chan

ISBN: 1502875640
ISBN 13: **9781502875648**
Library of Congress Control Number: **2014921776**
CreateSpace Independent Publishing Platform, North Charleston, SC

To Hayden and Kaitlyn

Thank you
Allen Yung and Henry Cheng
Without your encouragement this book would
never have been written

天下很多父母都梦想有个〝神奇秘方〞來教养自己的孩子，將一个婴儿变为一个快乐、行为端正的小孩，然後一个有成就、尊重他人的少年，最後是一个亲切和有信心的年青人。不过对很多父母来说，为人父母看來是噩梦多美梦少。

在这本书里，作者论述他们为人父母的经验。这个经验来源于他们养育的两个亲戚和朋友们都认为是〝成功〞的孩子，因为他们两个都是哈佛的毕业生和在事业上有成就的人。作者还认为学术上的成就只是成功教养的一个方面，同时还就教育方法对于他们自己来说是否有效做出了很坦率、很明确的评价，对此，他还用了他们孩子的评论和反馈作为辅助。

作者还在这本书里强调父母为了孩子好，不但要慎守自我牺牲和执行惩罚的规则，他还强调有效的教养会带来文凭不可替代的东西，那就是父母与孩子之间的爱、尊敬和感激。

Introduction

"How could all your children go to Harvard?" This is the question we have been asked repeatedly for years; too many of the people we know want to know. "It isn't just one but *all two* while ours have difficulties even get into a decent college, let alone Harvard." This is not an easy question to answer impromptu, and our answer is always like this: "We're lucky!" Yes, that is what a lot of people think we are, too, *plain lucky*!

Are we really? The answer is *yes* and *no*. Yes, in a way we are, because my wife and I are lucky enough to have each other as a very effective husband-wife team that can work together toward a common goal, and have two healthy and marginally smart children (two pieces of good material) for us to work on. No, it is not pure luck, there are something else: we have made tremendous efforts and sacrifices – we have spent nearly

Are We Lucky or What

引言

"你的两个孩子是怎样全部进入哈佛读书的？"这个问题这些年来不断地被问及，身边的很多朋友都想知道答案。"不是一个，而是两个全部去了哈佛；对于我们来说，能让一个孩子去著名大学读书就已经很不容易了，更不要说哈佛大学了！"如果没有事先的准备是很难回答这个问题的，所以我们的回答通常是"我们很幸运！"是的，很多人认为我们是幸运的，仅仅是幸运而已！

我们真的是这样么？答案是，也不是。在一方面我们是幸运的，因为我和我太太是一个非常有效的夫妻档，我们能相互协作朝着共同的目标不断前进，同时我们还有两个健康、比較聪明的孩子（两个可塑性很强的好材料）在另一方面，也不能仅仅归功于幸运，这里面还有一些其他的因素，譬如，我们做出了巨大的努力和极大的牺牲——我们几乎花了半生的时间并且用了不少钱来抚养他们。

half of our lives and a small fortune on rearing them. My wife had given up a promising career so that she could be a full-time mother and I had to scale back my business ambition in order to be a more involved father.

A Chinese friend we have recently made in China, who aspires to send his only son (10 years old) to Harvard, asked me for advice. He wanted to know our "secret recipes" of rearing two Harvard kids. Due to his persistence I told him what I thought we know, in a piece meal fashion, and only realized later I had not quite satisfied him, for he called me a few weeks later and suggested me to write a book. He wanted more detailed information. "A lot of parents want to know your secrets," he told me. "The book will sell like hot cakes in China."

Naturally, I turned him down, feeling offended in a way by his comment. *Selling like hot cakes!* What does he think I am, one of those money-hungry writers who would write anything including nonsense and

Are We Lucky or What

我太太放弃了前途光明的职业成为了一名全职妈妈；而我也不得不缩减自己在事业上的雄心壮志，以便更多地参与到父亲这个角色中来。

我们最近认识的一位中国朋友，他希望他唯一的，现在仅有十岁大的儿子将来可以考入哈佛大学，于是便向我们询问建议，希望我们能告诉他培养出两个哈佛学子的"秘方"。因为他的坚持不懈，终于，在一次聚会上，我简单告诉了他我认为知道的。不久之后，他意识到我说的那些并不能满足他，于是，几周之后，他拨通了我的电话，建议我写一本书，更加详细地介绍如何培养出哈佛孩子。他对我说："很多家长都想知道你的秘方，这本书在中国一定会热卖！"

当然我拒绝了他，因为他的话让我感觉受到了侮辱。一定会热卖？！他把我当成了什么，那些满身铜臭味的作家，为了几个臭钱，

garbage in order to make a few dollars? I am not like those who claim a lot but deliver little and who claim they are experts of this and that while they are nothing but opportunists. Besides, I do not believe we have any "secret formulas" of raising children and we certainly have never considered our two children going to Harvard is a *big* deal. There are hundreds of young people entering Harvard every year and not all Harvard graduates are successful or good citizens. Some of them would have been better off if they had gone to a trade school, learning to fix something and be useful. And I have never believed higher education (college and beyond) is for everybody; it should be reserved for those who wants to pursue teaching, research and other specialized professions. Basic education (up to high school) and learning a trade either from a trade school or on the job is sufficient for most of us to be useful. But keen competition for a decent job has raised the bar and misled us to believe that higher education will enhance our chances of success, which, in my opinion, is a fallacy. More than that,

什么垃圾、无聊的文字都能写出来的人？我不是那些华而不实的人，也不是那些自诩为专家，其实什么都不是的机会主义者。并且在养育孩子方面我们并不认为我们有什么"秘方"，也没有觉得两个孩子去了哈佛读书有什么大不了的。每年有成百上千的年轻人进入哈佛读书，可是不是所有的哈佛毕业生都会有所成就或者成为好公民。有些人更适合去职业学校，学习如何修理东西从而成为有贡献的人。我们也从不认为高等教育（大学及以上学历）适合所有的人，它只适合那些想在教育、研究及专业领域有所成就的人。基础教育（高中以下）加上从职业学校或者工作中学习到的一项专业技能足够我们当中的大多数人成为对社会有用的人。可是对于一份好工作的激烈竞争已经无形中提高了职业要求的准绳，并误导我们认为越高的教育将会增大我们成功的机会，在我看来，这些都是错误的。

after many more years of study, having loaded with student loans and emptied our parents' saving accounts, we cannot find the job for which we have been trained for. And at the end we either have to settle with a job that does not require a college degree or even worse, being unhappy, disenchanted and depressed, we are too proud to adjust. What a waste of money, time and human resource.

You may question us why we sent our two children to college and say college is not for everyone. Are we being biased and conceited, considering our children are superior to yours? Absolutely not! We had fallen into the same *trap*, too, for we were like everybody else, not knowing any better at the time. If we had known what we know now, we might have done differently and our children might not have gone to college at all. Fortunately, our ignorance had not become a mistake for us. But, not that many people are as lucky.

Anyway, let us go back to our friend who, embarrassed by my upsetting, quickly

Are We Lucky or What

更有甚者，在多年寒窗苦读之后，很多人用光了父母的积蓄还背负起了学生贷款，却找不到与所学专业相对口的工作，于是，便不得不退而求其次，去做一些根本不需要大学文凭的工作，甚至一些连高中的文凭都不需要的工作。由于之前太过于自信，以至于现在对所做的事情根本无法适应，于是便感到理想破灭、不开心、沮丧。这简直是对金钱、时间、人力的极度浪费.

你可能要问我，既然大学未必适合所有人，为什么我们还要把自己的两个孩子送进大学读书？难道我们是对他人存有偏见、瞧不起别人，觉得自己的孩子比别人的强？当然不是这样！想当初，我们和其他人的思考方式是一样的，并没有比别人多知道多少。如果当初我们有现在的想法，我们的做法可能会完全不同，两个孩子也有可能根本不会去大学读书。不过幸运的是，我们的无知并没有铸成大错，可是很多人却没有我们这样幸运。

好了，我们现在再回头说说我那位中国朋友，因为自己的建议冒犯了我感觉到很不好意思，

pointed out that I had misunderstood him. "Your two children not only have gone to Harvard but also are the nicest and the most successful young people I've ever known," he said. "What's wrong to help other parents doing the same thing as you and your wife have done?" Well, nothing is wrong with that and what he said about our children is *all true*. Besides, flattery is always music to the ear, to any ear.

But before commencing on this book, I want to make sure there is no objection from my family. On that, my two adult children are supportive primarily because they too are entering parenthood, and think the book can be a useful handbook for other young parents like themselves. However, we agree that if this book were to have real value for parents, then it is important for my children to provide a "response" to what I have to say about parenthood, since they are ultimately the ones who are on the receiving end of our parenting techniques. With the support and promise of cooperation from my children, I needed no

所以他很快地指出我误会了他的意思，并更正道：“你的两个孩子不仅去了哈佛大学读书，而且是我认识的最友善、最成功的年轻人。那为什么不帮助其他父母去做你和你太太做过的同样的事情？”好，他说的也不错，而且我的两个孩子也确实如此，并且赞美的话就如音乐一般，谁不愿意听呢。

　　但是在动笔写这本书之前，我还是希望确认一下家人并不反对这件事。我的两个现在已成年的孩子第一个赞成，因为他们也即将为人父，为人母，他们认为这本书对于像他们一样的年轻父母将会是一本非常有用的育儿手册。但是，我们想如果真的想要这本书货真价实，那么我们的孩子们就要对我们做父母的方法做出反馈，因为他们才是我们教育技巧的最终接受者。在两个孩子的支持和配合下，我不再犹豫，决定写这本书。

more persuasions and I decided to write the book. But the book I decided to write is not limited to teaching parents how to get their children into Harvard. It is intended to teach them how to be good parents and to raise good, successful children like ours. Getting into Harvard or any other elite universities is only a *byproduct* of good parenting. Other aspects, such as good manners, honesty, integrity, kind and loving, are far more important. They are the basic elements of success. We cannot be considered good parents if we fail to teach them any of these values. How can they be successful if their manners are so bad that nobody like them? How can we be proud of them if they do not respect and love us? What good are they to the society if they only take from it and do not give back? In another word, good parenting is all about nurturing and educating a child to become a good student, a good person and a productive citizen.

But writing a "how-to" book is very different from writing a novel; I only know

但是，我决定要写的这本书不是仅限于教家长如何使他们的孩子进入哈佛。而是更加倾向于教他们如何成为好父母，如何培养出像我们孩子一样品质优秀的、成功的孩子。进入哈佛或者其他名校读书只是成为好父母的一个副产品，而其他方面，譬如有教养、诚实、正直、有爱心，则更加重要。它们是成功的基本要素。如果我们没有教给孩子这些品质，我们就不能认为自己是好父母。如果他们没有教养，就没有人喜欢他们，那他们又怎么会成功呢？如果他们不尊敬、不爱我们，那他们又怎么能值得我们骄傲呢？如果他们只知索取、不知回报，又怎能成为对于社会有用的人？换句话说，好的父母就是培养和教育孩子成为好学生、好人和有用的人。

但是，写一本《如何……》的书和写一本小说是不同的。

how to write stories dreamed up in my head. They are not real and not based on facts. They are mere fantasies of my own creations. On the other hand, a how-to-do-it book is all based on facts, not fantasies. It must be true and honest or otherwise it may mislead our readers and do a lot of harm. We definitely want to make sure we, ourselves, are good parents and know our subjects well, and we must also have good children of our own to prove it.

Teaching parents to get their children into elite universities is not as simple as it seems. It involves so many things: student's own intelligence and ability, manners, sports, leadership, money, family background and, of course, *luck*. Yes, a lot of luck! Parents should know there are so many well-qualified students want to get into elite universities which have the luxury of pick-and-choose. What they are looking for are not book-worms who are good at only one thing and that is studying hard and making good grades. They have the responsibilities to look for and

我知道如何写出自己脑海中构思出来的故事。但这些故事不是真的，不是以事实为基础的。他们仅仅是虚构出来的、是我自己的创造。而写《如何…》这样一本书，是要基于事实，不是想象。它必须是真实、诚实的，否则它会误导我们的读者并产生很大的危害。因此，我们需要确定我们是一对好父母，对我们即将要讨论的主题有深刻了解，并且有很好的结果来证明它。

教家长如何将孩子送进名校并不是看起来那么简单。这里面有好多因素会影响它：学生自身的智商、个人能力、教养、所擅长的运动、领导才能、金钱、家庭背景，当然还有运气。是的，好多运气。家长们应该都知道每年有那么多符合条件的学生等着去名校念书，所以这些大学有太多太多的选择。他们不想要书呆子，只擅长做一件事，就是努力学习然后得到好成绩。他们有责任去寻找和教导未来的领导者，

educate future leaders – students who have a well-rounded ability and a good track record of leadership, and who will contribute to the good of human race and make a difference in this world.

For sure, there are other ways of getting into elite universities, which are much easier if you are super-rich, powerful, famous or dishonest enough to falsify your academic records. The super-rich can donate millions of dollars to the university and have their names on a building so that their offspring can be admitted without any problem. The powerful (children and grandchildren of kings, presidents and other political heavyweights), the well-connected and the famous can get in easily, too, without paying for it. For they are the ones that make a university famous and universities need them to perpetuate their elitism. The majority of us, who are neither rich nor powerful and nor famous, must work hard or be extremely talented to get in, except a few devious individuals who resort to dishonest tactics of fabricating fake academic

那些能力很全面，已经在领导才能上崭露头角的学生，正是这些人将会对人类做出贡献并且改变我们的世界。

当然，还有一些其他更容易的方式进入名校，譬如你很有钱，很有权或者很有名，又或者很不诚实地伪造了成绩单和社会活动。那些超级富豪可以捐赠巨款给学校，使他们的名字被刻在一些建筑物上，他们的后代也就会毫无疑问地被这个学校录取。那些有权力的人（国王、总统或者一些政治大佬们的孩子们或者孙子们）、背景雄厚的人、还有名人，他们进入这些名校也是很容易的，他们不需要为此付出任何东西，因为他们是那些会使这些大学更加知名的那群人，这些名校需要他们来延续自己的知名度。除了一些没道德的人，他们采用不诚实的方法伪造虚假成绩和课外活动成果。绝大多数的我们既没有钱、也没有权、也没有名气，需要靠自己的勤奋努力和天赋来考取这些名校。

records and extracurricular achievements. We are proud to say that our daughter and son did not need any of the above; they entered Harvard on their own merits.

In order to write a book that really can help parents; I had to work closely with my wife and our two children. We had to recall all the pertinent facts and every detail from the decades past, put them together and organize them in a way that makes sense to our readers. And importantly, for in-depth understanding and a well-rounded perspective for our readers, we included the feedbacks and comments from our children. Our goal is to present to our readers a *true account* of what we did and how we did it, including all the mistakes we have made along the way.

Like most parents we were very busy making a living and rearing children at the same time, and we had little time for planning ahead. We dealt with problems as they came up, one at a time, trying our best. Our readers must remember, this book is not a *Bible* of child-rearing and our way is not the *only* way.

我们可以非常自豪地说，我们的女儿和儿子并没有用到上述的任何一种方法，他们进入哈佛完全是凭借他们自身的條件。

为了能写出一本真正能帮助家长们的书，我不得不常常和我的太太和孩子们一起回忆十几二十年前的相关事件及其每个细节，并把它们组织整理好，使我们的读者更加容易理解。更重要的是，为了读者们能够有更加深刻及全方位的了解，我们还附上了孩子的反馈及评价。我们的目标是展现给各位一个真实的叙述，包括在此过程中我们犯了哪些错误。

像很多父母一样，我们一边忙着赚钱养家，一边教育孩子，几乎没什么事先计划的时间。基本上都是遇到问题了，才会尽自己最大的努力来解决问题，希望能够得到好的结果。读者朋友们，大家一定要记得，这本书不是一本教育孩子的圣经，我们的方法也不是唯一的。

There are so many different ways to raise a good child. Your child is as much different from ours as you are from us, and time and situations are not the same, too. The purpose of this book is simply to provide some ideas which we think will help parents take the *guess-works* out of parenting. However, your own discretion is advisable.

Finally, there is one more very important piece of advice: do not attempt to get your children into elite universities without rearing them to be a good person at the same time. It would not only waste your time and money in doing so but also would do more harm than good to the society. Remember the old saying: "*The higher it goes, the harder it falls?*" Rearing children is the same thing: the greater the sacrifice, the bigger the disappointment. Also remember, higher education is a two-edged sword, it can cut both ways. It can enhance the good but also can make the bad worse!

世上有很多的方法可以培养出一个好孩子了，您们的孩子和我们的是不同的个体，就像你们跟我们的不同一样。而且时间及环境也有差别。写这本书的目的就是给各位家长提供一些想法，希望它会帮助你们在教育的过程中除去一些猜想。不过还是请你们自作定夺。

最后，还有一个更重要的建议：如果在没有把你们的孩子培养成为一个好人时，请不要试图将他送进大学，这不仅是对你们时间和金钱上的浪费，更有可能对我们的社会造成危害。请记住这句老话：跳的越高，摔的越狠。培养孩子也是一样：你牺牲的越多，失望越大。同时也请记得，高学历是一把双刃剑，它可以使好的更好，也会使坏的更坏。

Be a prepared parent

You must have the maturity (not age) to be a good parent; you cannot be a kid yourself because a kid just cannot teach another kid. You will be surprised to know how many parents are kids themselves and very much unprepared to assume the role as a parent. We, too, were two of them. Only after we had a child of our own that we realized the need to prepare ourselves to be good parents. We started to read books about parenting, ask other parents questions and listen to their conversations with one another about their children. What we got out of all these was surprisingly similar. All said they put their children first and spent a lot of time with them. Generally, they bragged about their children endlessly. However, there was one advice we valued very much and it was from the Taiwan professor. It was a long time ago when I went there with a friend on business.

做一个有准备的父母

要想成为一个好父母，必须在心智上是成熟的（不是年龄），你自己不可以是一个孩子，因为一个孩子是不能教育另一个孩子的。你会感到很惊讶当你知道有多少父母自己都还是个孩子，根本没有准备好去承担一个家长的角色。我们也曾经是他们的一员。我们也是在有了自己的孩子之后，才意识到我们自己需要做好准备成为一对好的父母。我们开始读一些关于为人父母的书籍，向其他父母请教，倾听一些父母亲们有关于他们孩子的谈话。我们从中所得到的讯息惊人的相似，所有的父母都说把孩子放在第一位，并且花了很多时间和孩子们在一起。他们总是不停地夸耀自己的孩子。

但是有一条建议我们非常珍视，它是来自于一位台湾教授。很久以前我与一位朋友去台湾出差、他住在一位教授朋友家，

He stayed at his professor friend's apartment and I stayed at a hotel nearby. Every morning we had breakfast at the professor's apartment. One of these mornings while we were having breakfast, the professor's teenager son came to say good-morning to us and, to my surprise, asked my friend for permission to use the bathroom. A few minutes later, the professor's teenager daughter did the same thing. It was very unusual for a host to ask a guest if he could use his own bathroom. I was so impressed by the good manners of his children that I did not hesitate to ask the professor what was his secret of rearing such good children. After asking a few questions about my wife and me, he said to me, "If you're *stern* and *firm* and your wife *gentle* and *loving*, and you two don't argue and fight in front of your children and can work together as a team, you've nothing to worry about. You'll have good children." Since I had seen how good his children were, I took his advice seriously and followed it religiously – I assumed the "bad-guy" and my

而我住在附近的酒店里。每天早上我们在这位教授的家里吃早餐。有一天，当我们正在用餐的时候，这位教授十几岁的儿子过来跟我们打招呼，使我惊奇的是，他居然问我的朋友介不介意他使用一下洗手间。几分钟之后，这位教十几岁的女儿也做了同样的事。一个主人问客人是否可以使用他自己的洗手间，这件事非同寻常。他们孩子的良好教养给我留下了深刻的印象，所以我毫不犹豫地向这位教授请教培养出这么好的孩子的秘诀是什么。在问过几个关于我和我太太的问题后，他对我说："如果你很严格、坚决；你太太很随和、充满爱心，并且不在孩子面前争论吵架，如同一支队伍一样并肩作战，你们就没有什么好担心的，你们一定会养育出好孩子。"因为见到了他们的孩子是这么的好，我毫不犹豫地采纳了他的建议，并非常认真地按照他的话去做－－我扮演的是"坏人"，

wife the "good-guy" and we two opposite guys worked together as a team. I believe this arrangement has been a great help for us.

So, good parents need to provide love, guidance and discipline. But there is the problem, not many parents can provide all three adequately; more likely the one who is good at providing love is usually too soft and weak to provide discipline, and vice versa. Ideal parents should have one of them providing love (good-guy), and the other, discipline (bad-guy). Neither two "good-guys" nor two "bad-guys" make good parents. Love without discipline will *spoil* a child and discipline without love will *smother* him/her. The "good-guy" usually is the mother, should be gentle and soft so that she can yield, bend and blend in with her children; while the "bad-guy" (the father) should be stern and firm so that he can hold his position without wavering. Though it is easier for two different persons to assume the "good-guy" and "bad-guy" roles, a person (usually a single mother)

而我太太扮演的是"好人",两个相对立的角色齐心协力,我认为这给了我们很大的帮助。

所以,好的父母需要给孩子们爱、引导和约束。但是,这又出现了一个问题,很多家长不能适当地给予这三项。很多情况是,擅长提供爱的父母往往太软弱以致于不能提供约束,反之亦然。理想的父母亲应该是一方给予爱("好人"),另一方给予约束("坏人")。两个都是好人或者两个都是坏人都不能成为好的父母组合。没有约束的爱会惯坏一个孩子,而没有爱的约束也会抑制孩子们的发展。"好人",经常由妈妈来扮演,应该是温柔、和蔼的,这样,她可以对孩子适当地让步和孩子们打成一片;而"坏人"通常是爸爸,应该很严格、不妥协,这样才会稳住自己的观点不会来回摇摆。虽然两个人扮演对立的角色会比较简单一些,但是一个人(通常是单身妈妈),在这种特殊的情况下,如果自身有足够的不妥协的精神也是可以将两个角色演绎的很好的。

may, under unusual circumstance, perform both roles very well if she is tough enough.

But, providing guidance is a different matter; it takes maturity, experience and educated knowledge to guide a child onto the correct path. No guidance or wrong guidance will either make a child aimless, or worse, lead him/her in the wrong direction. Letting children develop on their own will never do; it is like letting someone operate a gun without giving him a proper lesson first. He might hit something by chance, but majority of the bullets would go astray. Some children might turn out fine or even great, but most of them would turn out disappointing – aimless, unmotivated, and lost in this world.

Fortunately, we are natural *good-guy-and-bad-guy* parents. The "good-guy", my wife, was born to be a great mother. She is gentle and kind, and she loves children, even if they have only one eye and no leg and as ugly as a toad. She has a genuine smile that is pleasant to every eye, a pair of ears that has plenty of patience for all the childish talks,

Are We Lucky or What

但是引导孩子却是完全不同的事儿，它需要父母的成熟、个人经历和教育背景来引导孩子走上正确的道路。没有或者错误的引导会使孩子失去方向，或者会使孩子误入歧途。让孩子自由发展是根本不可行的。这就好像让一个人在没有学习任何射击技术的情况下让他开枪射击一样，他可能靠运气会射中什么，但绝大部分的子弹都会不中目标被浪费掉。一些孩子可能会变得不错，甚者很好，但大多数会很失意——没有目标、没有动力、迷失在这个世界里。

我们很幸运，因为我们很自然地成为了"好人"和"坏人"组合的父母。好人，是我太太，她是一位天生的好妈妈，她很温柔、很和蔼，更重要的是她非常喜欢孩子，即使这个孩子只有一只眼睛，没有腿，还像癞蛤蟆一样丑。她有令每双眼睛都很愉悦的真诚的笑容，也有对孩子们的话充满耐心的耳朵，

and two gentle hands that can caress and tickle even a half-dead child back to life. Just the opposite, the "bad-guy," I, am naturally mean-looking, especially when I am not in a good mood. I am not particularly fond of children, especially those naughty ones. I find them annoying. And I do not think they like me either; they do not want to be near me nor do they want to have eye contacts with me.

In our family my wife is our children's loving mother, best friend, and the liaison between them and me. She gives supports and guidance, and always says it is my idea when discipline is needed. It works very well for us; it eliminates the necessity for confrontation between me and our children. I *control* them through a remote control, my wife.

However, nothing is better than keen observations of the behaviors of other parents and their children. We learn as much, if not more, from bad parents as from good parents. We can learn so much from their successes and failures, learn what to adopt and what to avoid, and in the process we may also learn a

还有一双温柔的手，可以爱抚、咯吱一个垂头丧气的孩子使他重新生气勃勃。相反的，坏人，是我，长得很严肃尤其是我心情不好的时候。我不是很喜欢孩子的，尤其是那些调皮的孩子。我觉得他们很讨厌。我也不认为他们会喜欢我；他们不想在我周围呆着，甚至都不想与我有眼神的交流。

　　在我们家，我的太太不仅是一位爱孩子们的妈妈，更是他们的好朋友，同时还是我和孩子们之间的纽带。她给予孩子们支持与引导，可是需要给他们立规矩时，她却常常说那是我的主意。这种方法很好，它消除了我和孩子们之间的正面冲突。我通过我太太这个遥控器来遥控他们。

　　但是，没有什么比热衷于观察其他父母与他们孩子的行为更好的方法了。我们从那些不称职的父母身上学到的一点都不比从好父母那里学到的少。从他们的成功与失败的经历中，我们知道了什么应该采纳、什么应该规避；同时也学到了一些关于自我提高的方法。

few things about self-improvement too. Look at the people around us, people we know very well, they are nice people and loving parents just like us, but they have lousy children. Why? Because they give their children too much love and not enough discipline. Instead of giving them an appropriate amount of love gradually, they give them too much too soon until they *spoil* them, just like an amateur gardener who gives too much water and fertilizer to a plant that he eventually *kills* it.

There is another way parents can ruin their children, they do a lot of scolding and make plenty of threats but little enforcements, because they are too soft and too loving. Instead of teaching, they would make all kinds of excuses for their children's bad behaviors, such as: "Nowadays, all kids are like that, all their friends are doing the same thing, or this is a different time now, we're out-of-date." We do not understand why they have to *follow* others. Can't they tell what is right and what is wrong? Even worse, when

再看看我们周围的人，我们的好朋友，他们也同我们一样，为人很和善、同样是充满爱心的父母，可是他们的孩子却不成器，这是为什么？那是因为他们给予孩子们太多的溺爱，却没有足够的规矩。他们在教育孩子们的过程中并没有逐步地、适量地施予他们爱，相反的却是太多、太急了，最终毁了孩子。这就如一个不专业的园丁，给了植物太多的水和肥料，植物承受不了那么多而死掉是一样的道理。

还有一项，如果家长们不注意会很容易毁掉他们的孩子。因为他们太没有原则、太溺爱孩子了，所以他们经常斥责、吓唬孩子，却很少将说过的话付诸实践。还有一些家长他们不去教育孩子如何做正确的事，反而不断地为孩子的坏行为找一些借口："现如今哪，其它孩子们都是这样的。"、或者"他们那些朋友们也都这样做。"、又或者"时代不同了，是我们自己落伍了。"使我们不明白的是为什么这些家长要按照别人的行为去要求自己的孩子，难道他们自己不能分清是非对错么？

they can tell what is wrong with their children and cannot tolerate them anymore, they would yell, "Can you stop that!" or "I've told you a thousand times and I'm not going to tell you again!" or "If you do it one more time, I'll skin you like a rabbit!" But, warning after warning and threat after threat, their children's unacceptable behaviors remain the same, because there is no disciplinary action rendered as promised. To their children all these half-hearted warnings, threats and yelling are only noises made by their frustrated, loving parents, and they do not bother them a bit. They have gotten used to them.

What they have not gotten used to are the harsh disciplinary actions such as spankings and other physical punishments, which may cause troubles down the road. When parents eventually cannot tolerate their children's bad behaviors anymore (usually happen when they are teenagers and no longer cute as babies) and get really angry and may have acted a little too violently, their children

可是当他们发觉孩子们有问题，然后忍无可忍的时候，他们便会朝着孩子大吼大叫："快停止这樣做！"、或者"我己经告诉了你一千次，我不会再 告诉你！"、又或者"如果你再敢做一次，我就扒了你的皮！"不断的警告、不断的吓唬，因为缺失 了与警告、吓唬相对应的惩罚行动，结果是孩子们那些坏毛病仍然是老样子。对于孩子们来说，这些"半真心"的警告、吓唬和吼叫只是来自于他们父母的聒噪，他们认为一直爱他们的爸爸妈妈只是因为他们不服管教而很有挫败感，并没有觉得爸爸妈妈是真的生气了，这对他们根本没什么影响，他们已经习惯了。

但他们不习惯的是警告之后的惩戒性措施，譬如打屁股还有一些其他的体罚措施等等，这将为以后带来更多的隐患。等到孩子们长到十几岁的年纪，不再像小时候那样可爱，家长们经常会因为无法再一次次的容忍孩子们的坏毛病而采取一些体罚措施，

would be stunned and feel the hurt too much to endure and may run away from home. There are thousands of such cases each year in America alone. This kind of tragedy can be avoided if parents are willing to prescribe bitter remedies to their children during earlier age. Let them taste the bitterness of the medicine and let them get used to the reality of disciplinary actions. For sooner or later they will have to.

To demonstrate my point I ought to tell you a real story. When my mother passed away and after her funeral we had a family gathering at our father's house. All my sisters and brothers were there, six of us. My oldest sister, who was 62 years old then, said our father was the cause of our mother's death, for he was too mean to her. At that, our father exploded and he slapped her face and then, smashed an ashtray with his bare hand and cut himself. As he was hollering at her and causing a thunder storm in the house, we all were as quiet and still as our mother's dead

他们的孩子因这样的行为而感到很震惊，没有办法接受，从而可能会离家出走。这样的案例单是美国每年就发生成百上千件。如果家长们愿意在孩子还小的时候便给他们一些苦口的良药，那这样的悲剧是完全可以避免的。让他们在小的时候就知道犯错的后果，那他们就会慢慢接受这些惩罚性措施存在的现实，因为这是迟早都是要接受的。

　　为了更好阐述我的观点，我给大家讲一个真实的故事。当年我母亲去世的时候，在参加完葬礼之后，我们六个兄弟姐妹就一起聚集在父亲家。当时 62 岁的大姐指责我们的爸爸：说妈妈的死都是由他一手造成的，他的脾气太暴躁了没有好好地待她。因为大姐的这句话，再加上妈妈辞世给父亲带来的极度悲伤，他突然过去扇了大姐一个耳光，然后用手砸碎了一个烟灰缸，碎掉的烟灰缸扎伤了他的手。可这并没有使他停下来，接下来他对大姐的斥责顿时在房间里掀起了一场大风暴，我们都不敢出声，乖乖的坐在那里一动不动，也没人敢过去帮他包扎伤口，

body, and nobody dared to help bandaging his hand until much later when he was calmed down by the bleeding. My oldest sister, embarrassed and ashamed, did not run away from the scene or our father's home. On the contrary, she showed her remorse by sitting next to him later during the dinner and constantly helping him with the food.

By today's standard, you may consider my father too violent. I am not condoning his conduct but his behavior would have been accepted as normal if we took into the consideration of the way and the time he was brought up. He had seen his uncle (57 years old and had three grandchildren already) who had offended his mother, knelled before her bed for many hours begging for forgiveness until she returned to the dinner table. My sister did not run away and did not have any resentment toward our father only because she had gotten used to this kind of punishment. And when you get used to something, it is a whole lot easier to accept. Of course, I am not advocating this kind of harsh punishment for

直到后来不断流血的伤口才慢慢地让他平静下来。即使这样，大姐都没有负气离开现场，更不要说推门而出了。反而她因为惹怒了父亲感到很后悔，在吃晚饭的时候还坐在父亲的旁边、帮他夹菜。

按照今天的标准，你可能会认为我父亲做的太过分，甚至有些残暴。我当然不赞同他的行为，但是如果按照当时他成长的时代和标准来评价他的话，他的那些行为是司空见惯可以被接受的。他曾经见过他的叔叔（当时已经有 57 岁，并且是三个孩子的爷爷了），因为冒犯了奶奶而跪在她的床前好几个钟头祈求她的原谅，直到她重新回到饭桌吃饭。我的大姐当时没有走开，也没有因此记恨父亲正是因为她已经习惯了父亲的这种发作方式。当你习惯某些事物时，你就会很容易接受它。当然，我不是主张对现在的孩子们用这种极端的惩罚方式，

children nowadays, but we do believe certain appropriate punishments are absolutely necessary as disciplinary tools. Children must learn to respect rules now at home and laws later in society. Perhaps we should make disciplinary actions a little more civilized, but we must have them.

We understand most parents have full time jobs; they have little time to spend on their children, and when they do have, they do not wish to spend it on discipline. They want to have fun together. It is good to be a fun parent, as long as you also show a serious side during times of discipline. Fun parent has to be able to be serious parent to get the child's respect for authority. This is also important to cultivate the child's sense of wanting to make their parents proud. But we do think that it is also important to build a multi-dimensional relationship with the child and let him/her develop affection for the parents and not just fear. It is fine to discipline a child for misbehavior, but be careful not to overdo it or do it publicly. Too much shame can make the

但是我相信适当的惩罚措施是立规矩的必要手段。孩子们必须先学会在家守纪律，之后再学会在社会上遵守法律。我们所需要做的是把这些惩罚性的措施更人性化一些，而不是把它们完全摒除掉。

我非常理解很多家长都是全职工作，很少有时间和孩子们待在一起。正因而此，他们就更不忍心将少的可怜的相处时间都花在给孩子立规矩上了。他们希望和孩子们愉快地相处。想与孩子做玩伴当然是件好事，只要你能在需要立规矩时展现出你严厉的一面即可。作为玩伴的父母必须也是严厉的父母，这样才会让孩子们树立对权威的尊重，培养孩子们希望自己成为父母的骄傲的意识。当然了，我认为发展全方位的亲子关系也是很重要的，我们不仅仅要让孩子害怕我们，也要让孩子们爱我们。因为孩子的行为不端而惩罚他/她是可以的，但要注意的是，不要做的太过，或者在公共场合不顾孩子的颜面。

child lose self-confidence and resent the parent. It is easy to be a fun parent; anybody can be his/her child's best friend, but that is not enough to be a good parent.

But, no parents are worse than the ignorant and the obsessive parents. They are not fit to be parents. The ignorant parents (it has nothing to do with the level of education) are those who either have no common sense or have difficulty in learning. They believe all kinds of absurdities without thinking and not even consider the reliability of their sources. I know such a person who has an M.B.A. degree, but believed what an illiterate old woman told her, and ate a lot of pig brains during her pregnancy, thinking pig brains would make her baby smarter. It is laughable! For any person with common sense should know, if pig brain can do any good at all, at best it can only make a child as smart as a pig! There are more laughable nonsenses: some mothers believe playing multi-language audio tapes to unborn babies would enable them to speak many languages, and flipping a

过多的羞辱会使孩子失去自信、憎恨父母。成为一个玩伴式的父母再简单不过了，任何人都可以成为他/她孩子的好朋友，但是这对成为一名合格的父母是远远不够的。

最糟糕的两种父母：一种是愚昧无知的，另一种是过分关注孩子的，这样的人不适合做父母。所谓愚昧无知的父母（与所受教育程度无关）就是那些毫无常识或者对学习有困难的那些人。他们从不思考一下就相信那些荒唐的不合常理的事情、也不考虑这些消息来源的可靠性。我就认识这样一个人，还是从商学院毕业的硕士生，居然相信一个文盲老太太对她说的，怀孕的时候吃猪脑，可以使孩子更聪明。这简直太可笑了！有常识的人都知道，如果吃猪脑有用的话，最好的结果是会使这个孩子像猪一样聪明！还有一些更好笑的事情：有些人相信在怀孕的时候，给肚子里的宝宝听多种语言的声带会使宝宝讲多种语言；

book – just flipping and not reading – would make them literary writers; they also believe having a child holding an ice cube for hours would build his/her endurance for pains and hardships and locking him/her in a dark room would build courage.

Alas, we believe none of these! However, we believe the physical and emotional state of a mother has a great impact on an unborn baby. During pregnancy my wife did not drink coffee, tea or alcoholic beverage but drank milk, ate healthy food, and walked a lot to keep healthy. She also kept herself stress free by staying away from unpleasant things but doing those things and going to those places that would make her happy. It is quite logical that a healthy and happy mother should have a healthy and happy child.

The obsessive parents are sick people themselves and they need psychological helps. They love their children so much that they have difficulty distinguishing rights from wrongs and often cross the blurry line without

快速地翻书－－只是翻，不是阅读－－会使孩子成为作家；还有让孩子手握冰块几个小时可以锻炼他们对疼痛和困难的忍耐力；把孩子锁在黑屋里可以锻炼他们的勇气。

我们完全不相信这些！但是，我们认为怀孕时妈妈的身体和精神状态对胎儿有很大的影响。在怀孕期间，我太太从不喝咖啡、茶、酒精饮品，而是多喝牛奶、吃健康的食物、经常散步。在我的帮助下，让她远离那些不开心的事情、做她喜欢的事儿、去会使她开心的地方，不要让她有任何压力。

而那些过分关心孩子的父母，他们自身就是有心理疾病，需要心理上的帮助。他们太爱他们的孩子以至于区分不出对与错，经常做过了头却浑然不知。

knowing it. I have seen a parent who let her child urinate on the floor of a posh department store because she believed a five-minute walk to the restroom would be too long for her daughter to hold and thus would damage her bladder; I have known a parent who thought the dormitory of a major university was not clean enough for her child; and I have heard a parent who said that carrying a backpack of a few books and walking fifteen minutes to school would hurt the back of her 20-year-old daughter. She should have seen our children carrying thirty pounds of golf clubs and walking for hours playing golf when they were in their early teen.

We also understand that not all mothers can afford to stay home to take care of their own children; they have to go to work and leave the duty of child-rearing to others, such as nannies or day care centers. These are not ideal alternatives, simply because they, the professional caretakers, cannot provide the same level of attention and love to the child as a mother can. Consequently, the child feels

我曾经见过一位家长让她的孩子在一间豪华商场的地毯上小便，因为她觉得要走 5 分钟去厕所对于她女儿来说时间太长了，会憋坏她的膀胱；我还认识一位家长，她觉得大学的宿舍太脏，根本不适合她的孩子住；还有一位家长，她说背着装了几本书的书包走路 15 分钟去学校，会伤了她 20 岁女儿的背。她真应该看看，我们的孩子们早在他们十几岁的时候，因为打高尔夫，得背着 30 磅重（大概 27 斤多）的球具，在球场上一走就是几个小时。

　　我们也很理解，不是所有的妈妈都有一定的经济基础可以让自己呆在家里全心全意地照顾孩子。她们不得不去工作，只能把养育孩子的事情交给保姆或者幼儿园。我觉得这不是理想的解决办法，原因很简单，他们这些专门看小孩的保姆或者阿姨不可能给予每个孩子同等的关注与关爱。这样做的后果就是，孩子们觉得自己被忽略了、不被大家喜爱，这正是导致日后孩子逆反的最关键因素。

neglected and unloved which are the two major causes of defiant and hostile behavior.

But, there are always ways to mitigate this situation if parents are willing to sacrifice a little. They can take turns to care for their child by one working day shift and the other night shift, so that there is always one parent at home with the child. Or they have to make do with one income and forget about other luxuries for a while. We have friends did just that and their children turned out fine.

Since we both were born and raised in China but live and educated in America, we have been exposed to two drastically different cultures, the old and the new, which all have their pros and cons. But fortunate for us, I grew up in an environment that I could not trust people easily and, as a result, I have been accustomed to doing a lot of evaluations before adopting something new or eliminating something old. We are both conservatives and unlike most people of our generation, we do not fall to fashions and fads, believe in those

但是如果家长们愿意牺牲一点点的话，我们总会找到更好的解决办法。譬如一个上日班，另一个上夜班，这样总会有一个人在家陪伴着孩子；亦或者干脆留一个人在家全职照顾孩子，那我们就只能暂时忘记那些奢侈的东西，靠一个人的收入生活。我们有一些朋友就是这样做的，他们的孩子也成人长進。

我和太太都是在中国出生长大，然后到美国求学生活，所以接触到了旧式的和新式的两种截然不同的文化，它们都有各自的优点及缺点。但是我很幸运的是，我成长的环境使我养成了不轻易相信别人的习惯，所以我经常在接受新事物，摒弃旧事物之前会做很多相关的评估。跟很多我们这代人不同，我和太太都是很保守的，不喜欢追时髦、赶时尚，也不相信那些明星代言的广告，更不会头脑简单地盲目听从朋友和邻居。

star-sponsored advertisements and listen to our friends and neighbors simple-mindedly.

Feedbacks and Comments:

Marcie: Our mother is always very supportive; she gives us plenty of freedom to do whatever we like. There were only a few times when she did not agree with us and would say, "You better not do it because your father might not allow it." Then, she would explain to us the reason for our father's objection. She not only makes us understand our mistakes, but also removes our resentment towards our father and increases our respect for his wisdom.

Although our mother always dressed us nicely, she seldom bought us brand name clothes. She always says, "What's outside doesn't matter, it's what's inside that counts." Perhaps that was why I never envied other girls wearing fashionable dresses and brand name shoes, and all my good friends in high

孩子们的反馈和评论：

玛诗：妈妈一直都是我们的支持者，无论我们想做什么她都会给予我们充分的自由去尝试。仅有几次她和我们的想法不一致，并规劝我们说："你们最好不要去做，因为爸爸是不会同意的。"然后向我们解释爸爸反对的原因。她不仅使我们明白了自己犯的错误，而且还消除了我们对爸爸的不满情绪，使我们更加敬佩爸爸的睿智。

虽然妈妈总是把我们打扮的很得体，但她从来不给我们买名牌衣服。她经常跟我们说："一个人的外在美并不重要，重要的是他的内在美！"这可能就是我从不羡慕那些穿着名牌衣服和鞋子的女孩子的原因。我中学和大学的好朋友都是好学生，从不是什么时尚模特！

school and college were good students, not fashion models. My conservative attire had also saved me a lot of trouble – no boys dared to ask me for a date.

Garwin: As of a couple months ago, I became a father myself as my wife and I welcome our son, Hayden, into the family. I know my dad is a very strong advocate of the "good guy/bad guy" approach, but this is something that I'm sure I will struggle with myself as Hayden gets older. Unlike my dad, I actually like children and I think children tend to find me more fun than terrifying. After a long business trip, I can't wait to get home and give my son a hug and play with him. And to be honest, part of me also wonders if my life would have turned out that much differently if my dad had been a bit more *friend* and a bit less *disciplinarian*. I'll never really know the answer to that riddle, but for now, I'd like to believe that I can adapt my dad's approach to fit my own personality and my own family's circumstances. So I do share

我的那些保守的穿着也帮我解决了好些麻烦 ——
没有男生敢问我是否想跟他出去约会。

家荣：两个月前，我和太太迎来了我们第一个
孩子，陈劲兆，自己也当了爸爸。我知道爸爸是
非常赞同这个"好人和坏人"的方法，可是随着
劲兆逐渐长大，我可能对这个做法有所保留。跟
爸爸不同的是，我本身是个很喜欢孩子的人，我
觉得孩子会喜欢亲近我，而不是害怕我。在一次
很长时间的出差后，我恨不得马上飞回家抱抱我
的儿子和他一起玩。说实话，有时候我在想，如
果爸爸能再和蔼一点，在立规矩上再少那么一点
点严格，那么我的人生会不会完全不同呢？这个
是个永远没有办法回答的问题，但至少现在就我
个人的性格和我们的家庭情况而言爸爸的方法还
是很适合我的。

my dad's sentiment, that there is more than one way to raise a child, and I may try some variations to the approach that I was raised myself. However, I do support my dad's belief that ingraining discipline into a child's psyche and standing firm on what's right versus wrong is important in any setting. So if one day I do have to choose between being a disciplinarian or friend to my son, then I'll gladly sacrifice my son's friendship for his respect in order to be an effective parent.

我也很赞同爸爸的另一个观点，养育孩子的方法不止一种，我倒是很愿意去尝试一些不同的方法培育劲兆。但有一点是不容改变的，那就是要给孩子树立规矩，在任何情况下都要坚持正确的毫不动摇。所以如果有一天我需要在一个严厉的父亲和朋友式的爸爸之间做出一个抉择的话，那我会很乐意牺牲我们的友谊来做一个令他敬畏的爸爸。

Never too early to teach

One major mistake most parents make is that they *postpone* teaching their children until they reach the age when they start showing disagreeable behaviors. They all think babies are too young to learn, too cute to talk to them harshly, and too lovable not to cater to all their whims. "We'll teach them *later*," they always say. "There'll be plenty of time for that." But, they are wrong because learning ability, according to many reliable, independent studies, diminishes with age. Innocent babies score the highest. They are capable of learning almost anything, including multiple languages.

We started training our children right after they were born. Breast feeding was the very first step. It establishes an everlasting bond between a child and its mother. (Prviding the mother is healthy and has good milk. Never squeeze the milk into a bottle and

教育孩子从小抓起

教育孩子最常出现的问题就是很多家长延迟教育，直到孩子们出现一些不尽如人意的行为才着手实施。我们总认为婴儿太小了，学不会什么；他们又太可爱了，所以讲话的时候不能太严厉了；他们也太招人喜欢了，实在不忍心拂了他们的意愿。"我们等等再教他们也不迟。"家长们总是这样说，"以后教育他们的时候多着呢。"等等。这些想法都是错误的，根据许多研究证明，学习的能力会随着年龄的增长而逐渐减少。那些天真无邪的小婴儿往往能力最强，他们几乎可以学会任何事，包括多种语言。

我们在孩子一出生就开始训练他们。第一步是母乳喂养，它会帮助妈妈和孩子建立起一个永恒的纽带。（如果妈妈的身体健康，奶水的品质也很好就不要把母乳挤出来然后再用奶瓶喂孩子，而是直接吸吮妈妈的乳房，这是母乳喂养的最关键步骤。）

feed the baby later with it. Sucking a mother's breast is the most important part of breast feeding.) Then we talked to them, touched them, caressed them, tickled them and made them smile, which was another step to establish a loving relationship with our children. After that we started toilet-training (not only kept them cleaner but also gave them the first lesson to learn), we taught them to entertain themselves by giving them toys, taught them good manners by cheering them on for their good behaviors and punishing them for bad ones. Once I hit our son's little hand when I caught him tearing wall papers off the wall. I did not hit him hard, of course, but he got the message and never did it again. As a result, our children always behaved well. They seldom cried and whined (it is a child's way of getting attention) and we ignored them if they did. They never ran around and threw forks and knives in restaurant like many children do. We could take them to weddings and concerts without having to worry about getting embarrassed by them.

然后我们开始和他们聊天、触摸他们、爱抚他们、咯吱他们和逗他们笑，这些是下一个步骤。这样就可以与孩子们建立起充满爱的和谐关系。接下来便是训练他们如厕（这不仅可以让孩子们更干净，而且也是他们人生的第一堂课。）然后是给他们一些玩具让他们学着自己玩；教他们懂礼貌，做的好的时候会讲一些赞扬的话，做的不好会受到惩罚。譬如有一次我正好撞见儿子在撕墙上的壁纸，我就打了他几下手板以示惩罚。当然我并没有打的很重，但是他得到了讯息，爸爸不允许这样，所以他以后就再也没有做过了。这样做下来的结果是，我们的孩子行为举止非常好。他们从不哭闹（这通常是孩子们引起大人注意的方法），如果他们这样做时，我们是决不理会他们的。他们从来没有像很多孩子那样在餐厅里到处乱跑，随便乱扔餐具；我们可以经常带他们参加婚礼和音乐会，从不担心他们的行为会使我们尴尬。

Well-behaved children have additional advantages. Because they behave well, they tend to be well liked and to draw rather than expel quality adults. They spend more time listening and interacting with us adults than children who do not behave well, and consequently, they learn a lot more from us about everything, from daily life to special knowledge. Not like other children who are screaming and running around playing their own silly games, our children always sat still and listened while we had a conversation and they often participated in it.

Many people admire us, for our children are not only well-behaved, good students and good golfers, but also fluent in Chinese, which is almost impossible for an ABC (American Born Chinese). They all wonder how we manage to succeed while they fail. What they do not know is that I have a wise father. He forbade us speaking Cantonese (common language in Hong Kong) at home and made us speak our native tongues, *Hakka*, unless we had visitors who

Are We Lucky or What

行为举止良好的孩子还会有其他的受益。因为我们的孩子表现良好，大家很喜欢亲近他们，所以大人经常把他们留在身边，而不是赶他们去一边玩，因此他们就有更多的机会听大人们聊天、与大人们交流，从他们那里学到很多东西，小到日常生活大到专业知识。。在其他的孩子还在大呼小叫、疯跑、玩游戏的时候，我们的孩子已经可以静静地坐在那里倾听大人们谈话，并且经常参与到其中来了。

很多人羡慕我们，因为我们的孩子不仅举止得体，还是好学生，好的高尔夫球运动员，而且讲中文讲的又很好，这对在美国出生的华裔来说几乎是不可能的。所以他们很想知道我们是如何成功地做到的。他们不知道我有一个多么明智的爸爸。那时候他禁止我们在家里讲广东话（当时广东话在香港是通用的语言），我们必须讲我们的家乡话（客家话），除非家里有不会讲客家话的客人。

could not speak ours. As a result, we all could speak our own dialect besides Cantonese while most immigrant children could not. Remembering that and thought it was a good idea, we adopted my father's dictatorial approach and applied it to our children. As expected, it *worked!* They now can speak both Chinese (two dialects: Cantonese and Mandarin) and English fluently.

But this kind of dictatorial approach is not for every parent, they must be tough enough to ignore the resentment from their children and do not mind to hurt them a little, at least for now. For sure they would not like it just as we did not like it when our father forced it on us. Here is the biggest difference between good and bad parents. Good parents' loves for their children are for the *long-term*. Whatever they think is good for their children's future, they would pursue it until it is done, and sometimes it means to hurt and make their children miserable right now. But most parents do not have the hard hearts to do so; they can't bear to see their children suffer

于是，我们除了会讲广东话之外，还会讲我们的家乡话，而很多移民到香港的孩子都不会讲自己的家乡话。想起这些，我觉得这是一个很好的点子，所以我就复制了父亲这个霸道的方法，并用到了我孩子的身上。正如我所预期的，这个方法很管用！他们的中英文讲得都很流利。

　　但是这个霸道的方法并不适用于每个家长，他们必须足够坚定来忽略来自孩子们的不满，并且不介意小小地伤害一下孩子的情感，至少在执行期间会如此，因为我可以非常肯定孩子们并不喜欢这样，就像当初我们不喜欢父亲把这个要求强加到我们身上一样。好的父母对孩子的爱是有远见性的，无论什么，只要他们认为对孩子的将来有好处，他们都会坚定不移地朝着这个方向不断前进，即使当时这种做法对他们的孩子有小小的伤害或者使孩子并不好过。但是大多数的爸爸妈妈硬不起心肠来这样做，因为他们不忍心看着孩子难过，他们的情感阻碍了他们预见到孩子们未来将要遭受的磨难。

and their emotions prevent them from foreseeing their sufferings down the road.

I remember when we were touring the western part of China, a couple who had two very spoiled teenagers asked me why ours behaved so well and what advices I could give them to improve theirs. I wished I could tell them honestly, "My friends, it's too late. Nothing you can do about it now." But I kept my mouth sealed and smiled instead. Why hurt someone who has already been hurt.

The primary reason why our children behave so well is because we have trained them well and *very early*. Not as other people think: they were born that way. We molded them into the shapes we liked. We strongly believed that the earlier they were under our influence, the less chance they would be affected by the bad influences of outside elements, such as peer pressure, TV, school and neighborhood. Not only we trained them early, but also made sure we did it correctly because we would not have a *second* chance.

Are We Lucky or What

　　我还记得有一次我们去中国的西部旅行，一对团友夫妇，他们的两个孩子都十几岁了，却被惯的不像样子，于是便问我为什么我们的两个孩子表现的那么好，还请我给他们一些建议如何去改善他们的孩子。我当时真想告诉他们实话："朋友，太晚了，现如今你什么都做不了了！"可是我什么都没说，以笑代之。我为什么还要伤害那些已经受伤的人呢。

　　我的孩子们行为举止如此好的最主要原因是我们在非常早的时候就开始训练他们。并不像其他人那样认为：他们天生如此。我们按照自己认为对的方向去塑造他们，并且十分坚信这种塑造越早开始，我们对孩子的影响力就越大，外界的不良因素，譬如同龄人、电视、学校以及邻里邻居等等，对他们的影响力就越小。所以我们不仅要尽早开始，更要确定我们的方向是正确的，因为我们不会有第二次机会。

We divided our duties; I was responsible for disciplinary actions and my wife handled the rest. She made learning fun for our children and made sure they had a sound foundation before they started school. She motivated them so they would study by themselves without any push from us, talked to them, met their friends, and tried to understand their feelings and thinking. She also taught them good manners, humbleness and not to be a materialistic person, taught them those good eating habits and how to stay healthy, and even taught them to respect time and not be habitually late. But most important of all, she made our home warm and loving for them.

And because good manners and good habits are the two very important traits that affect a person's future, we had paid more attention to them, down to tedious details. We taught our children not only good manners, always smiling and respectful to others, but also good habits. We taught them to be on time regardless the degree of importance of

Are We Lucky or What

我和太太分工合作：我负责立规矩，而太太负责其他的。她会寓教于乐，使孩子们开心地学会了好多知识，所以他们在上学前便有了很好的基础；之后她又不断地激励他们使他们能够自发地学习不需要我们的督促；她还经常和孩子们聊天，见他们的朋友以此来更好地了解他们的情感及想法；她还教孩子们要懂礼貌、谦虚、为人不能功利，还有帮助他们养成良好的饮食习惯，保持健康，甚至还教他们要尊重时间，不要经常迟到。但是最重要的是，她使我们的家既温暖又充满爱。

因为懂礼貌和好的行为习惯是影响一个人未来发展的最重要的两个因素，因此我们也非常重视孩子们这两点的培养，尤其是一些细节方面。我们不仅教育孩子要懂礼貌，见到他人要微笑、要尊敬他人；还教导他们要有好的行为习惯，不论这个约会重要与否都要守时，

the meeting, habitual lateness is an apparent form of disrespectfulness for others and the easiest way to offend and lose a friend or a job. We taught them to be neat and clean, be generous, and eager to help. All these small things would make a big difference in determining whether they are likable or not. And we taught them by setting examples ourselves; when we stay at other people's house, my wife always helps with the cooking and I always do the dishes and set the table even though I seldom do these things at home.

Our teaching did not *stop* when our children left home for college. Almost every evening after dinner my wife and I took a walk together around the pool for an hour or so, to talk about our children. My wife would tell me everything about them and if there were problems that she could not solve by herself, I would make some suggestions. It worked extremely well because our children talked to her every day on the phone when they were away at Harvard, and through her I

经常迟到很明显是对别人的不尊重，会使我们很容易冒犯或者失去朋友，甚至是工作。还有在家的时候要保持家里干净整洁，到别人家拜访要大方得体，有眼力见儿，能帮人家做些力所能及的事情。所有这些小事情都会决定着他们是否会被别人喜欢，是否会受到大家的欢迎。我们的方法是以身作则，当我们在别人家做客时，我太太经常帮助主人在厨房里打打下手，我呢就帮忙摆桌子、洗碗，虽然这些事情我在家里很少干。

　　我们对孩子们的教育并没有因为他们离开家上了大学而停止。几乎每天晚上吃完晚饭，我和太太都要绕着泳池散步一个小时，同时聊一聊孩子们的事情。她会把孩子们的所有事都讲给我听，如果遇到什么解决不了的问题，我就会给她一些建议。这个方法很好，因为每天她都要跟在哈佛读书的孩子们通电话，通过她，我能很清楚地了解孩子们的近况。

was well informed, too. Occasionally, when my wife did not agree with my suggestions which she thought too harsh for our children, I normally would give in and let her handle it alone, for I knew without her motherly love I would have driven our children away from home long time ago.

Feedbacks and Comments:

Marcie: In order to ensure my brother and I were able to speak fluent Chinese (most American born Chinese cannot), my father adopted his father's method – to mandate speaking Chinese only at home unless we had guests who are not Chinese. My brother and I even had to argue in Chinese. Despite a few unhappy instances like these, which we were too young to realize the value of them, our home was the happiest and the warmest place on earth. I felt I had all the freedom I ever wanted. My brother and I were never pushed

有时候，太太不同意我的建议，觉得我的方法太
苛刻了，那我就会让步，让她自己用自己的方法
解决，因为我知道，如果没有她这个妈妈的爱，
我的孩子们可能早就远离这个家了。

孩子们的反馈和评论：

玛诗：为了让我和弟弟能说一口流利的中文（
很多在美国出生长大的华裔子女都做不到），我
爸爸采用了爷爷的方法－－要求我们在家里只能
说中文，除非有不会讲中文的客人在。甚至有时
候我和弟弟争吵也得用中文！尽管那时候有这样
一些小的不愉快，因为我们当时还太小不能认识
到这样做的好处，可是我们的家是世界上最快乐
最温馨的地方。我觉得在家里我可以得到我想要
的自由。爸爸妈妈从来不督促我们学习，

to study, seldom had our requests denied, and we were even free to take the money that was so casually left in the drawers without asking, though, we always asked.

Garwin: In terms of teaching and nurturing children at an early stage, I very much believe that my father's view is fundamentally correct, and quite frankly, it's not a very controversial concept. What more debatable, however, is *how* to teach and *what* outcomes one should expect to receive from one's children. While my parents employed similar techniques and teaching approaches for my sister and me, we are nevertheless two very different people (gender-related differences aside), even though we share the same value that our parents tried so hard to pass on to us. My sister is overly detail-oriented, while I am overly lackadaisical. She's overtly friendly, while I am reluctantly social. She excelled mostly in class, while I excelled mostly at exams. The point is, everyone is different, so the key is to start early to identify your child's strengths and personality and foster an attitude in which they strive to learn and to improve. Fostering that mentality to *want to*

很少拒绝我们的请求，他们甚至还允许我们不需要询问，随时取用放在抽屉里的零用钱，但是，我们总是在问过父母之后才会去拿。

家荣：就教育培养孩子从小抓起这一点上，我认为爸爸的想法毫无争议，完全正确。但是如何教养孩子以及我们应该对孩子有怎样的期待是需要我们来探讨的。虽然父母在我和姐姐身上用了相似的教育技巧和方法，又教给了我们相同的价值观，但是排除性别差异不说，我和姐姐是两个完全不同的个体。姐姐她非常细心，而我总是懒洋洋的；她为人很热情，而我却不太喜欢交际；她在课堂上表现的很出色，而我是考试成绩很出色。每个人都不同，所以关键点是我们要尽早开始来确认孩子的个人实力、性格特点，然后帮助他们形成一种努力奋斗和自我提升的态度。在心理上形成渴望自我提升、学习的态度是爸爸教育理念的最关键一点。

improve and learn is the biggest key to my father's message. That's where active parenting is most useful. To set parameters for what is appropriate behavior and effort, parents need to be both role models and mentors to their children.

How to do so is also the more debatable subject. The main role of the disciplinarian is to instruct and enforce. It is not to be a confidante or a friend. I often wonder if effective nurturing can be achieved if it is coming from a parent who is both a disciplinarian and a friend. Honestly, I don't know, but I think most would agree that it is tempting to try. But similar to my sentiments in the previous chapter, for the sake of the child, it's probably better to err on the side of disciplinarian over friend. It's better to install a belief in the child that they can be better behaved and get better grades than other children because they are unique. I grew up believing that I had to get straight-A's and that belief ties directly to how my parents set a very high bar that we needed to achieve. I'm sure if my parents just said, "It is fine, you tried your best already to get that B-minus," I

在这一点上，需要父母充分发挥积极的引导作用。至于在限定孩子适当的行为界限上，家长们不仅需要给予适当的指导，并且要以身作则。

至于"如何来做"则是更具争议的话题。一个作为立规矩的人，主要的角色是指导者和实施者，不是知己，也不是朋友。我时常在想，如果 父母可以身兼立规矩的人，以及朋友这两个角色，那教育的效果是否会更好。说实话，我不知道，但我很确定的是这是很值得一试的事情。但是跟我前一章的观点相似，若是为了孩子，必须在两个角色中选一个的话，严格立规矩的父母显然要好过朋友式的父母。我们还要给孩子们灌输这样一个信念：他们可以比别人做的更好、取得更好的成绩因为他们是与众不同的。我从小就自信我是一个全 A 生，这样的想法当然与我父母给我设定的非常高的标准是密不可分的。我坚信，如果爸爸妈妈对我说："虽然你得了 B-，但是你已经尽力了，没关系的。" 我想我就不会有这种为了成功而奋斗的精神了。

don't think I would have had the same drive to succeed.

War at home

Unless you train your children early and train them well, you will otherwise have an on-going war with them, and turn your home into a battlefield. You can imagine the anguish and frustration of the constant arguing with and yelling at your children when they are openly defying you, the banging of doors and locking themselves in the room when they do not want to hear from you anymore and, if they are bolder, they may run away from home and make you to call the police to find them. Fortunately, we never had such problems; our home was always peaceful and cheerful. All we heard was the sound of music, the joyful laughter or the soft dialogue between our children and their mother.

That is why we urge parents to train their children early, for it is so much easier to raise children if you have a good head start – to get them to behave well, obey and respect

家庭战争

除非你很早就开始教育你的孩子，并且教育的很好，否则的话，你会一直和他们斗争下去，家就变成了硝烟弥漫的战场。你可以想象一下，因为长期不断的争吵而产生的苦闷与烦躁；因为孩子公然违背你的意愿，你对他们的大吼大叫；还有因为不想听到你声音，他们重重地摔上了门，把自己反锁在房间里等等。如果他们胆子足够大，他们就会离家出走，让你不得不叫来警察帮忙寻找他们。幸运的是，我们从来没有遇到这样的问题，我们的家一直都是宁静快乐的。我们听到的永远是音乐声，欢笑声，还有孩子们和妈妈轻柔的聊天声。

这就是为什么我们非常希望家长要尽早开始教育你的孩子，如果你开了一个好头，那么你教他们良好的行为习惯、服从尊敬你、清楚明白你的要求，这些自然会事半功倍。

you, and know your rules. But what if your children do not behave well and do not listen to you, is it too late to do anything? No! It will never be too late to train a child, but it will be a lot tougher. If your children are still young (below 8), all you need to do is to have a firm grip on them and do not let them get away with anything. Give your children plenty of explanations and guidance first, followed with warnings (not threats), and if they still ignore your warnings, you must administer the disciplinary actions that you have promised them. Never underestimate your children, they are clever little devils. They know how to manipulate parents to go against each other and to get one of them on their side. Both parents must unite and never contradict each other. Like a country, it can never win the war if the government and the people are divided.

We all know disciplinary action may not work on all children or all the time. Like a prescription, it must be the right medicine and the right dose for it to work. It is deplorable

但是如果你的孩子行为习惯不好，又不听你的话，那是不是就太晚了，什么都做不了了呢？当然不是！教育孩子没有太晚，只是可能更困难而已。如果你的孩子还不到 8 岁，那么你需要做的事情就是牢牢地掌控他们，不让他们偏离你既定的方向。首先要给孩子充分的解释及引导，接下来给予适当的警告（不是吓唬），如果他们无视你的警告，那么你就要施予之前警告的惩戒。也不要低估你的孩子，他们是聪明的小恶魔，他们知道如何能让爸爸妈妈意见相左，然后把一方拉到他的战线上来。所以各位爸爸妈妈你们要团结一致，不要在孩子面前相互反对对方，这就像一个国家，如果政府和人民不齐心协力，是没有办法赢得战争的胜利的。

　　我们都知道惩罚措施不是对所有孩子、在任何时候都有效的。就如一份处方药，必须对症下药并且剂量得当才能发挥作用。

that some parents punish their children by suspending their allowances, exercising house imprisonment or no TV and video games for a week. Why should their children care about these things anyway; they have plenty of money in their piggy banks and they can always talk to their friends on the phones. To make the disciplinary action work, it must be severe enough and hit them where it hurts the most. It can be anything depending on the child and the situation. For our children, the most severe and effective punishment would be for their mother not speaking to them. "You're not nice; I don't want to talk to you." These few words said in an angry tone were enough to make them behave. How could they not feel hurt and frightened if they lose their best friend and the colossal column of support?

Very rarely did I have to confront our children. Only when they were not nice to their mother that I had to holler at them with angry face, "I don't care you're nice to me or not, but I cannot permit you not nice to your

有些家长通过不给孩子零用钱、不让他们出门、不许看电视、不许打游戏来惩罚他们，我觉得这些做法很可笑。孩子们为什么要在意这些？他们的存钱罐里有好多零用钱；不许出门，他们可以在电话里和朋友聊天。如果我们想这个惩罚措施有效，那么它必须要足够严厉而且能够击在孩子的痛处。至于具体是怎样的措施那要依孩子和当时的情况再来定夺。对于我们的孩子，最严厉以及最有效的惩罚莫过于他们的妈妈很生气地跟他们说："你们表现的这么不好，我不想跟你们说话了！"这简简单单的一句话足可以使孩子们乖乖听话。如果他们失去了最好的朋友、最大的支持者，他们又怎么能不害怕呢？

　　我基本上很少与孩子发生正面冲突。只有在他们对妈妈很不礼貌的时候我才会板起脸大声喝止住他们。"我不在乎你们是不是对我很友善，但是妈妈为了你们付出了一生的心血，

mother, for she's sacrificed her whole life for you guys!" Like a rod my words hit them on the head and woke them up from the daze of emotion that had temporarily controlled them. They have good reasons to be afraid of me; aside from my frightening facial expression, I have a reputation as a rough person who has a quick temper with zero tolerance and has no consideration for consequence.

Once I left two naughty nephews of my wife on the shoulder of a lonely road to punish them (to scare them really) for ignoring my warnings, and I drove off for miles until their mothers cried in panic and begged me to go back. Another time I took a bunch of naughty kids who came visiting with their families to the front yard of our house and showed them the big spiky tree. I had each of them touch the spikes and feel the sharpness. They did and laughed, thought it was fun until they heard my stern warning: "If I see you guys horse around and scream again, I'll strip off all your clothes and have you hug this tree and I'll tie you to it with a

我绝不允许你们对她这样没礼貌！"我的话会给他们当头一棒，足可以使他们从暂时的不理智情绪中清醒过来。除了那张一发起火来吓人的表情不说，我那火爆、毫无耐性，以及不计后果的脾气，会使他们非常害怕我。

有一次太太的两个侄子因为无视我的警告，在车上调皮捣蛋，所以我就把他们扔在一条清静公路的旁邊以示惩罚（只是想嚇唬他们），开了几英里之后，在他们妈妈哭着请求后才回去接上他们。还有一次，一群顽皮的孩子随着他们的家人来我家做客，我把他们带到前院，让他们看了一棵带刺的树，还让他们摸了摸上面尖尖的刺。开始时他们都觉得很好玩，之后便听到我严厉的警告："如果你们再到处乱跑、大声吵嚷，我就脱光你们的衣服，把你们绑在树上一个小时，让你们好好体会一下抱着它的感觉！"

rope for one hour." Laughter stopped abruptly and they went away trembling. Ever since, they behaved like ladies and gentlemen, at least in my presence, until one day at a dinner party at our golf club. They were so excited about something that they had forgotten my warning. They were screaming and running around and chasing one another among tables until I seized the leader and asked him, "Have you forgotten the tree I showed you the other day?" That simple! Peace was restored without another word.

Of course, not everyone agrees with my way of teaching, even if it works. They think it is too harsh, too cruel and too inhumane. They say it may damage a child's self-esteem and restrict its creativity. They prefer the way of permissiveness – to let a child run wild and develop on its own. If their farfetched theory holds truth and parents' guidance, teaching, and discipline are not needed in a child's development, then, we should have no need for parents, teachers, mentors, and prisons. Well, everybody is entitled to their opinions.

于是笑声嘎然而止，一个个惨白着小脸跑掉了。从那以后一个个俨然成了绅士、淑女的模样，至少是我在场时是这样的。直到有一次在高尔夫球俱乐部的晚宴上，他们不知为什么太兴奋了，显然是忘记了我的警告。他们高声叫喊着，在餐桌间相互追逐嬉笑打闹，直到我逮到了带头的孩子，然后问他："你忘记了我给你看的那颗树啦？"看，多简单！都不需要多说一个字。安静的环境又重新回来了。

当然，即使结果是好的，可是对于我的教育方法却是仁者见仁，智者见智。他们认为我的方法太极端、太残酷也太不人道，这样会毁了孩子的自尊、限制了他们的创造力和心理的正常发展。他们更喜欢那种"散养"的教育方法，让孩子们顺其自然的发展。如果这样的理论是正碩的，那么在孩子的成长过程中，根本不需要家长的引导和影响，以后自然也不需要老师、学校，甚至监狱了。每个人都有权保留他的意见，

This is a free world after all. But I can assure you, there is no such thing as free lunch; you either have to pay for it now or pay for it later. And we prefer to pay for it now. For it is much easier, once and for all, to train our children to behave well at the very beginning than to *fight* them for the rest of our lives.

Feedbacks and Comments:

Marcie: I am proud to say that our home is a heaven, not a battlefield. I seldom gave my parents any troubles. The few times when I retorted my mother, due to childish emotion, and made her angry, I regretted it immediately and apologized to her. Nothing is more painful for me than to see my mother unhappy because of me.

Garwin: My own son is now a lively 6-month old baby. A bundle of joy in many ways, but like other babies, this bundle of joy

毕竟这是一个自由的世界。但是我要告诉你，世上没有免费的午餐：你早晚是要付饭钱的。现在付了，就容易很多，一次全部付清，现在教育好孩子，以后就享享清闲，否则你将会一路和他们斗争下去。

孩子们的反馈和评论：

玛诗：我可以非常自豪地说我的家不是战场，而是天堂。我很少给爸爸妈妈找麻烦，仅有几次，因为那时候还很孩子气，妈妈批评我的时候我跟她回嘴，惹得她很生气，不过事后我立刻就后悔了，然后会向她道歉。没有什么会使我看到妈妈因我而生气感到更难过的了。

家荣：我的儿子现在 6 个月大，很可爱。但是也像其他宝宝一样，有些小问题。

can also be quite a handful. In his case, my son likes to be cuddled to sleep, and if my wife or I simply set him in his bassinet hoping he falls asleep on his own, he'll let out such a fit that we'll quickly regret our hasty move. It must be my parents' influence subconsciously creeping in, I have started to train our child early and have him comfort himself to sleep and not rely on us grownups to coddle him to sleep. Already, I can see that this "discipline" thing will not be easy! But I will try to follow in my parents' example and have the resolution to discipline my child for his future benefit.

我的儿子喜欢让我们抱着入睡，如果我和太太把他放到婴儿床里让他自己入睡，他就会因为我们的离去而放声大哭。可能是爸爸妈妈的做法对我产生了影响，我很早就开始训练我的儿子，希望他能安抚自己，不需要大人抱着，可以自己入睡。但是我已经看到了，这个规矩执行起来并不是那么容易！不过为了儿子的将来，我还会尽我所能按照父母的方法来管教他。

Give children the opportunity

Like farming, parenting is a full time job and an art. Good parents not only need to have the basic knowledge of parenting but also have to pay full attentions to their children. Like farmers who must *balance* the needs of their crops – they will die if they are not given enough water, sunlight and fertilizer, and they will also die if they are given too much of them – parents must do the same for their children. They must decide how much love to give, how hard to push them and in what direction, how firm with them and how much freedom they should have, etc. Although their children will not die if they do not do it right, they certainly will be *spoiled or neglected* and become rotten.

We started testing our children very early, when they were babies, to find out their strengths and weaknesses. One of our favorite

给孩子尝试的机会

家长的工作，就如同种田一样，是一个全天的工作，同时也是一门艺术。好的父母不仅需要拥有做家长的基本知识，还要非常关注他们的孩子。就像农民必须要平衡作物所需的养料－－如果他们没有被给予充足的水、阳光、养料，他们就会死掉；如果他们被给予的过多，仍然也会死掉－－家长们对孩子也必须做同样的事情。爸爸妈妈们必须决定到底要给孩子多少宠爱、我们需要用多大的力量来督促他们前进，同时前进的方向在哪里、还有严格管理他们严格到什么程度，给他们自由又自由到什么程度，等等。虽然孩子们不会因为我们做的不对而像作物一样死掉，但是他们一定会因为溺爱或者忽视而被毁掉。

我们在孩子们还是小婴儿的时候就开始测试他们，以此来找出他们强项和弱项。

tests was to give them a photograph of a hotel hallway with its white ceiling, white floor, and two white walls with nothing on them but two rows of door on both sides. It was not easy to tell even for us adults whether it was upside-down or sideway. When our 8-month-old daughter was given the photograph, she always turned it to its proper position, every single time, no matter in what position we had given her. "Wow, what a *smart* girl!" my wife and I would cry out excitedly with pride. But when our son, also 8-month-old at the time, was given the same photograph, he did nothing to it. He held the photograph exactly in the same position as he was given, every single time, too. "What a *dummy* boy!" my wife and I would cry out dejectedly with disappointment.

But we had not given up on him. He was such a nice boy; never cried and never whined, even would watch his sister skate for hours without a fuss. One day, we discovered he wrote his Chinese name in reverse, which is hard to do even for us. We suspected our

Are We Lucky or What

我们最喜欢的一种测试方法是给他们看一张图片，这张图片照的是一个酒店的走廊，白色的天花板、白色的地面和白色的墙面，墙上除了两侧各有一排门什么都没有。这幅图对于大人来说都很难分辨出是上下放颠倒了，还是左右放颠倒了，但是每当我们把这个图片给我们八个月大的女儿看时，无论是以什么方位给她，她总能把它转到正确的方位。"哇，多聪明的孩子啊！"每次我和太太总能因为无比的骄傲激动得热泪盈眶。但是到了我们的儿子，也是八个月大，给他一样的图片，他却什么都不做，只是拿着，按照我们给他的那个方位，动都不动。"这孩子也太笨了吧！"我和太太每次都因为失望而沮丧的要命。

但是我们从没有放弃过他，他是那么一个好孩子，从不哭闹，甚至看姐姐练习滑冰好几个钟头都不闹。直到有一天，我们发现他完全反着写自己的中文名字，这对成年人来说都是很困难的事情，

son could see things a normal person has difficulty seeing. To prove that we gave him a picture of a duck in upside-down; he called out immediately without turning: "Duck." Then, we gave me a picture of a lion in sideway; he called out: "Lion." We were so happy that we were holding each other crying with joy. Our son is not dumb at all!

We really believe all children are gifted. They are born to be good at certain things; some are good at sports, some at music, and some at science and so on. As parents we must try our best to find out what our children are good at and do our best to give them the opportunities to develop their talents. Of course, not all parents are as fortunate as we are, who can afford to give our children the opportunities to try out many things, including piano, ice skating, dancing, singing, and golf; but there are many other things that are free or cost little. They only need to have the desires.

But be cautious when you provide your children the opportunities, always make sure

所以我们猜想他有可能会看到一个正常人很难看到的事物。为了证明我们的猜想，我们给了他一张上下放颠倒了的鸭子的图片，他没有把它搬正，却很快说出了："鸭子！"，接着我们又给了他一张左右放颠倒了的狮子的图片，他会很快叫出："狮子！"我们太高兴了，我和太太抱头痛哭，我们的儿子一点都不笨！

所以我们坚信所有的孩子都是有天赋的，他们一定在某个方面很擅长，可能有的擅长体育、有的擅长音乐、有的擅长科技等等。做为家长，我们必须尽我们所能来发现孩子擅长什么，并且尽最大的努力给我们的孩子创造机会去发展他们的才华。当然，不是所有的父母都如我们这般幸运，有足够的经济实力给孩子机会去尝试很多东西，例如，钢琴、滑冰、跳舞、唱歌、还有高尔夫。但是，还有好多东西是免费或者花费很少的，我们需要的仅是有这样的想法去让孩子尝试。

当你给孩子们提供机会的时候要多加小心，

your children will benefit from them in a positive way. Do not lavish them with material stuffs such as expensive toys, newest gadgets and brand name clothing; just because you can afford them. We know some friends who not only gave their children their own rooms equipped with computers, color TVs, stereo systems, but also cellular phones and trendy cars (if they are old enough to drive). We can see why. They are either too soft and could not refuse their children's requests or want to make up to them for the guilt of not be able to spend more time with them or simply want to show off their successes through their children. With so many distractions and toys to consume their time, the result is very much predictable.

On the contrary, we had made sure our children did not spend our money and their time wastefully. They had no cellular phones and computers of their own until they went to college. At home, we had only one computer in the living room for all of us to share. We let them drive (to school only) only after they

Are We Lucky or What

一定要确保孩子们能从中获得积极的、正向的东西。如果仅仅是因为你买得起，那么就请不要过分给予孩子物质上的满足，譬如，昂贵的玩具、最新的小玩意、名牌的衣服，等等。我们的一些朋友，不仅给他们孩子们的房间装上了电脑、电视、音响，还给他们买了手机、甚至一成年就买了汽车。我们知道他们为什么会这样，因为他们太没有原则了，不会拒绝孩子们的请求，或者因为没有时间陪伴孩子便想在物质上弥补他们，又或者仅仅是想通过孩子来炫耀他们的成功。有这么多的东西来分散孩子们的注意力和时间，那结果可想而知。

相反的，我们不允许我们的孩子浪费我们金钱和他们的时间。他们直到上大学才有自己的手机和电脑，在家的时候，他们只有客厅里的一台公用电脑可以使用；在他们可以证明自己是合格的、有责任感的司机之后，

had proved they were good and responsible drivers. But we were not parsimonious on their books, golf equipment, golf lessons and tournament travels, of which we thought would benefit them in life.

Feedbacks and Comments:

Marcie: Our parents exposed us to many different things in order to discover our interests/talents. They would not go to places without us; we traveled with them extensively, ate out often and, more importantly, we had the opportunity to mingle with their friends and business associates and observe the ways our parents treated them. We learnt a lot by osmosis.

Garwin: As a child I always envied other kids who had video games and water guns, but when I finally had them only after repeated pleading to our loving mother, I would play with the new toys a few times and

我们才允许他们自己开车去学校。可是在书籍、高尔夫球具、请高尔夫教练、参加比赛上我们是从不吝惜的，因为我们觉得这是对他们的发展有帮助的。

孩子们的反馈及评论：

玛诗：爸爸妈妈用了好多不同的方法来发现我们的兴趣和天赋。他们不会把我和弟弟留在家里自己出门，反而是带着我们游历过好多地方，经常一起外出吃饭，更重要的是，我们还可以参加他们与朋友以及生意上合作伙伴的聚会，使我们有机会观察爸爸妈妈待人接物的方式，在潜移默化中学会了很多。

家荣：作为一个孩子，我总是羡慕其他的孩子有电子游戏、水枪玩，所以我求了妈妈好多次，最终拥有它们，但是在玩了几次之后，

very quickly find them boring and never touch them again. Our father is right; most toys are waste of money and time. He is not a frugal though; he spent generously on other things that he thought would benefit us in the long run. He bought us expensive golf equipment, took us to concerts and museums, hired us golf coaches, travelled with us, and let us order from regular menu instead of kiddy's menu, which other parents would probably consider a waste of money. The opportunities that our parents had provided us proved to be very valuable.

我便没有了新鲜感，不再玩了。所以爸爸是对的：绝大多数的玩具都是浪费钱和时间。他并不是一个节俭的人，他可以在一些对我们的发展有帮助的事情上很慷慨，譬如给我们买很贵的高尔夫球具、请高尔夫教练、带我们去音乐会和博物馆、和我们一起旅行、给我们点成人餐而不是儿童餐，很多这些别人认为是浪费钱的事情。事实证明爸爸妈妈给我们提供的这些机会都是很有价值的。

Set high standards

Maybe because I have a demanding father who had constantly pushed me to the limit, I have become a *demanding person* myself; I not only demand a lot from myself but also from our children. I demanded them to be good kids, good students and good athletes. I remember when our daughter showed me her first grade report, I took a look (it was all A's) and said, "Good, from now on you don't have to show me any more reports until you get a B." That was the *only* report I ever saw from our children because both of them were straight A students.

I also remember the first time we were invited to an honor-students-of-the-month luncheon sponsored by our daughter's middle school, we were amazed to see parents and grand-parents bring flowers for their love ones, feeling very proud of them. Later we found out honor students are not straight A

立高标准

可能是因为我有一位要求很高的父亲，他总是不断地把我们推向极限，久而久之，自己也成了一个要求很高的人，我不仅仅这样要求自己，同时也这样要求我的孩子们。我希望他们是好孩子、好学生、好运动员。我还记得女儿上小学后第一次拿回来成绩单给我看，上面全是 A，我看后就跟她说："很好，以后就不用给我看了，除非你考了 B。"这是唯一的一次我看他们的成绩单，因为他们两个都是全 A 生。

还有一次，那是第一次被女儿的初中邀请，去参加他们为荣誉生所举行的午宴。我们惊奇地看到，不仅仅是父母，甚至爷爷奶奶都有来参加，他们手捧鲜花送给他们可爱的孩子，感觉是那么的骄傲和自豪。后来我们才知道，荣誉学生并不是我们想的都是全 A 生，

students as we had expected, any student with a B average or better is an honor student. If our children got a B, we would have brought a cane for them, not flowers. We just do not understand why so many parents set their expectations so low. We believe parents should set *high standards* for their children, the higher the better, so their children know what are expected of them and give them something to shoot at.

Yes, we set very high expectations for our children, but that does not mean we demand them to live up to our expectations and express disappointment when they do not. High expectations are only goals we set to encourage them to work harder, try harder and get more satisfactions out of their efforts and achievements. We would have been just as satisfied and proud of them if they were unable to fulfil our expectations as long as they had tried their best.

平均成绩在 B 以上就可以了。如果我们的孩子成绩是 B，那我根本不会送他们什么鲜花，而是藤条！我们实在没有办法理解为什么这么多的家长们把他们的期望设置的如此低。相反的，我认为家长应该给孩子订立高标准，越高越好。这样，孩子们知道他们需要达到什么样的标准，这会让他们更有前进的目标。

是的，我们给两个孩子设定了很高的期望值，但这并不意味着他们一定要达到我们的期望，我们更加不会因为他们达不到而表现出失望的神情。高标准只是一个目标，鼓励着他们勤奋努力、不断尝试，通过自己的不断努力和进取，取得更满意的成果。即使孩子们不能完全达到我们的期望，只要他们尽了自己最大的努力，我们还是会因此而感到满意和自豪的。

Feedbacks and Comments:

Marcie: I never had problem with my parents' high expectations. I always tried my best to fulfil them and make my parents proud of me. It has become a habit for me. Even today, without my parents setting high expectations for me, I set them for myself in order to push myself to try my best.

Garwin: I know my dad is only being humorous when he mentioned that he would take out a cane if we ever came home with a "B". To be honest, I don't really remember ever being punished for receiving a bad grade on a test. I do remember once in 6th grade when I failed a written quiz (on the rules of dodge ball or something similarly random and useless) for my physical education class because I was absent a few days before for a golf tournament and did not know about the test. It's quite embarrassing to reflect on it now, but I remember that I actually cried when my mom arrived at school that day to

孩子们的反馈和评论：

玛诗：对于爸妈的高标准，我从没有让他们失望过。我总是尽自己最大的努力去实现它，使爸爸妈妈感到非常的自豪。现如今，这已经成为了一种习惯。即使今天，他们不再为我订立什么很高的目标，可是我自己会设定一个，为的就是能让自己全力以赴。

家榮：我知道爸爸只是幽默而已当他提到：如果我们的成绩得了 B，他就会拿出藤条教训我们。说实话，我真的不记得自己因为考试成绩糟糕而被爸爸惩罚过。记得 6 年级的时候，有一次因为参加高尔夫球锦标赛而缺了几天的课，并不知道有测验，所以回来上学那天的体育课笔试小测（关于躲避球规则或是其他类似的内容）就没有合格。现在说起这件事还会觉得很不好意思，但是我记得妈妈那天放学来接我的时候我哭了。

pick me up. I remember thinking how unfair it was to have a blemish on my otherwise spotless report card because of a stupid test for PE class. More than 20 years later, I still recall how my mom accompanied me to see the teacher and how shocked he was that a parent and child would go see him after hours to discuss how I could retake the test (as it turns out, the failed quiz stood but I was still able to get an A in the class). The important thing to take away from this otherwise irrelevant event is that somehow, my parents were able to instill into my sister and me an internal drive to be excellent and hold ourselves to a high standard. That 11-year old Garwin didn't cry because he feared punishment, but because he hated the feeling of failing. Another key part of this story is that my mother was there to get me through it and never even hinted at punishment. So setting high standards for your child is important, but so is being there to give him all the support necessary for him to succeed and believe in himself.

Are We Lucky or What

我觉得因为一个体育课的小测使我完美无瑕的成绩单上有了一个污点，这简直太不公平了。20 年后的今天，我仍然能回忆起妈妈是如何陪着我去找老师的，当时老师又是多么惊讶，放了学家长会陪着学生过来商讨如何补考的事情（结果是，那个不合格的小测还在，不过我仍然可以在这个科目上取得 A 的成绩）。从这件事和一些其他的事情上我们可以得出的结论是，不知道我的父母是怎样给我和姐姐灌输了自我要求的高标准和追求十全十美的动力的。11 岁的家荣哭泣的原因并不是因为害怕惩罚，而是不喜欢失败的感觉。这件事的另一个关键就是我的妈妈一直陪在我的身边帮助我，从没有暗示过要惩罚我。为你的孩子设定高标准是很重要的，但是更加重要的是你要陪在他的身边，随时准备为他的成功并自信提供必要的帮助。

Identify and solve problems

Rearing children is *never* a smooth sailing; it always has problems. But problems can be minimized and solved if parents are vigilant. Here are a few examples of problems that we had with our children and how we dealt with them.

Problem 1: Our daughter came home crying after the first day at school. She told us kids at school made fun of her and she did not like going to school here in America. She wanted to go to school in Hong Kong. We knew it was not a racial issue, for we strongly believed innocent kindergarten kids could not possibly be racially motivated. They were too young to know the ugliness of racial discrimination. They made fun of her because she was the *only* Asian at a school of predominantly White and Hispanic, and she did not yet speak good English – she spoke Chinese at home and had spent a lot of time in

发现问题、解决问题

养育孩子并不是一帆风顺的，我们经常会遇到很多问题。但是如果父母们可以时刻保持警惕，那么我们就可以将问题缩小并解决。下面就是我们孩子遇到的几个问题，以及我们是如何解决的它们的。

问题 1：我们的女儿第一天去学前班，放学的时候哭着回来跟我们说，学校里的小朋友取笑她，她不喜欢在美国上学，她想回香港上学。我们知道这不是一个种族歧视问题，因为我们相信学前班的孩子还是很天真的年纪，不可能有种族主义的概念，他们还太小不能理解什么是种族歧视。他们取笑我们的女儿，可能是因为在白人和西班牙裔占主导的学校里，她是唯一一个亚裔孩子，再加上她的英文说的又不好－－她在家里讲中文，

Hong Kong. We believed her problem was a psychological one. She lacked self-confidence and thus felt intimidated.

She was not the only one that had this kind of problem; most immigrant children encounter the same situation. They are teased for their homemade lunches that they bring to school, for their clothes or hair styles, and for their accents and other ethnic features. Many parents act passively; they choose to live in their own ethnic communities, so their children can go to a school where most of the students are of the same race. But, there is a problem: they cannot assimilate into our society easily because they lack the opportunity to interact with people other than their own. They have not solved the problem; they merely prolong it until the day when their children have to step into mainstream America.

Solution: But we acted proactively; we confronted the problem head on, once and for all. We sat our daughter down and *convinced* her that she was so much more superior to the

又在香港呆了很长一段时间，所以我们更觉得她的问题是一个心理问题，她缺乏自信，所以对学校产生恐惧感。

　　她不是唯一一个遇到这样问题的孩子，大多数移民的孩子都有类似的问题。他们可能会因为自带的午餐、着装、发型、口音或者其他一些种族特征而被别的孩子取笑。很多家长对此的反应都很消极，他们会选择住在自己种族的社区，这样孩子周围的同学就大多都是一个族裔的了。但是这样就会出现另外一个问题：这些孩子很难融入我们的社会，因为除了跟他们一样的人，他们很少有机会接触其他类的人。所以，这些家长们并没有解决问题，而是将问题推迟到了他们的孩子不得不融入美国主流社会的时候而已。

　　解决方法：我们要积极主动地面对问题、解决问题。我们先让她坐下来，然后慢慢地说服她，使她相信她比好多孩子都优秀，

other kids at school because she could speak two languages, had travelled to so many places and had a nice home and loving parents. "You should make fun of them, not the other way around," we told her. After that she was not only the best student at school, year after year, but also a very popular one too.

Problem 2: Many years later, we discovered our son also had a problem, but a different kind of problem, the kind that is exactly *opposite* to our daughter's. He became very cocky and he looked down on other kids who were not as good as he was at school or at golf. We tracked down the *root* of the problem and that was: he and another boy who was two years older dominated the local junior golf tournaments. They were the only two that always fought for the first place. The reason for their dominance was clear: our son had a private coach and a private club to practice and play golf and the other boy also had plenty of opportunities to practice and play, because his father was a teaching pro,

因为她可以讲两种语言，又去过好多地方，还有一个温暖的家和爱她的爸爸妈妈。我们告诉她："你应该取笑他们，而不是被他们取笑。"从那之后，她不仅仅每年都是学校里最优秀的学生，也是非常受欢迎的一个。

问题 2：许多年之后，我们发现儿子也出了问题，但是是完全不同的问题，跟他姐姐的问题完全相反。他开始越来越傲慢，看不起那些在学习上和在高尔夫上不如他的孩子们。我们寻根究源，终于让我们发现，那是因为他和另外一个大他两岁的男孩雄霸了当地所有高尔夫青少年锦标赛，冠军的位子几乎只是由他们两个相互争夺。原因很简单：我们的儿子有私人教练和俱乐部来练习高尔夫；而另外一个孩子也有很多的机会练习，因为他爸爸是一家高尔夫球场的教练。

managing a golf club. But other local kids were not as fortunate; they had neither teachers other than their fathers, nor private clubs to sharpen their games.

Solution: We started *limiting* our daughter and son's participation in golf tournaments of Temecula Valley Junior Golf Association (TVJGA) and had they joined the Southern California Junior Golf Association (SCJGA) which is one of the biggest junior golf chapters in the country, with a large pool of top-notched junior golfers and where Tiger Woods was a member. At SCJGA, the standard is very high and the competition very keen, because most its junior golfers either aspired themselves or being pushed by their parents to be college or professional golfers. They all had coaches and some even had sports psychologists.

For the first few tournaments our son did poorly, almost at the bottom, and it was something he had never experienced before. He hung his head and wanted to cry after the tournament and we, as parents, watching him

其他的孩子就没有那么幸运了，他们除了老爸，既没有教练、更没有私人俱乐部来练球。

解决方法：我们开始限制女儿和儿子参加由我们当地梅蒂丘拉谷青少年高尔夫球协会（TVJGA）举办的锦标赛，然后转向参加南加州青少年高尔夫球协会（SCJGA），这是美国最大的青少年高尔夫球协会之一，拥有很多顶尖的青少年高尔夫球选手，老虎·伍兹就曾经是这里的一员。在这里球技水准非常高，比赛竞争也很激烈，因为这里面的绝大多数选手都是立志，或者被家长们期待着能成为大学校队的选手，或者职业高尔夫球运动员。他们全部都有自己的私人教练，有的甚至还有自己的心理医生。

最初的几场比赛下来，儿子的成绩很糟糕，几乎是垫底儿的，这是他从来没有经历过的，他耷拉着脑袋，看起来都要哭了。作为父母的，

defeated and dejected wanted to cry, too. But, we had to endure the sufferings of his defeat which, we believe, was necessary in order to make him a *better* person, a humbler person. Fortunately, our children have a gentle, caring and loving mother to whom they can always go for comfort and encouragement. She would make all kinds of excuses for them not doing well – Oh, you never played this golf course before or there are just too many good junior golfers here. And at the end she always patted fondly on their shoulders and said, "Next time you'll do better, won't you?" They would nod, feeling much better already. A shot in the arm!

From always a winner to always a loser and from trophy holder to trophy admirer was enough humiliation for our son; he did not need the added disgrace from us to stimulate him to work harder on his golf game. He constantly work on his swing and putting, even at home before going to bed (evidenced by the many barren spots on the carpet in his bedroom) and, as a result, he moved up the

看着他挫败、垂头丧气，我们也很难过，但是我们不得不咬牙挺住，因为我们知道，这是他成长为一个更优秀的人、更谦虚的人所必须经历的。幸运的是，我的孩子们有一位和蔼、善解人意、爱他们的妈妈，她总是在他们的身边不断地安慰并鼓励着他们。她会为他们失利找各种各样的理由，譬如，你从没在这个高尔夫球场打过球，又或者，这儿好选手太多了，最后，她还会怜爱地拍拍孩子们的肩头说："下一次，你们会打的更好，是不是？"孩子们会点点头，情绪忽然好得多了，仿佛打了一针兴奋剂一样。

从常胜将军到失败者，从奖杯的拥有者到奖杯的渴望者，对于儿子来说这已经是奇耻大辱了，他根本不需要再从我们这得到更多的羞辱来刺激他在高尔夫上要更加努力。他拼命地练习挥杆，即使在晚上睡觉前也是如此（因为经常练习，他房间的地毯都被他磨平了），结果是，他的成绩上升的很快，

rank quickly and eventually won a few tournaments. He was not a dominant golfer at SCJGA as he was at TVJGA and he had not brought home many trophies. Neither had he had a "big head" on his shoulders any more.

Actually, our children gave us very little problems comparing to other children; we had avoided most of the problems associated with children by carefully selecting the right kind of neighborhood they would live in, school they would go to, and screening their friends they would play with. We moved from the haughty Newport Beach of the rich and famous to the much humbler Temecula of the working class; we chose public school for them instead of private school, even though we could afford it, so that they would not pick up those arrogant behaviors from spoiled rich kids and could mingle comfortably with ordinary ones. And we had eliminated peer pressures, which are very bad for children and cause parents to lose control of them, by confining them at home, school and the golf course, and keeping them

最终赢得了几次锦标赛的胜利。在 SCJGA 这个圈子里，他不能像在 TVJGA 那样的占优势，也没有那么多的奖杯带回家，但是，他已不再是那个骄傲的少年了。

　　事实上，较之其他孩子，我们的孩子基本上很少有问题，因为我们已经有意识地规避了一些潜在的风险。为了他们，我们很慎重地挑选与什么样的人做邻居，他们要去什么样的学校念书，也很仔细地筛查过与他们一起玩耍的朋友。我们从声名在外的富人和名人聚居地，新港，搬到了名不见经传的工薪阶层聚居地，蒂梅丘拉；即使我们可以负担的起私立学校，却放弃了它，选择了公立学校，这样他们就不会从那些被惯坏的富家子弟身上学到骄娇二气，可以和普通人很好地交往；同时，我们也为了排除来自同龄人对他们的影响——这种影响很不好，容易使家长失去对孩子的控制——把他们限制在家里、学校和高尔夫球场之间，

very busy with homework, golf and travel. It does not mean they were *deprived* of friends and social lives and missed out on the fun of growing up. On the contrary, we think they were much happier than most children. At school, teachers and staffs liked them because they were good students and polite kids; at our golf club, members admired their beautiful golf swings and good manners, and they liked to socialize with them; and at home, we seldom needed to scold them and tell them what to do. We gave them all the freedom they wanted and let them do whatever they pleased, for they rarely would do something we did not approve.

Feedbacks and Comments:

Marcie: I was too young, and it was such a long time ago to remember what had actually happened the first day at kindergarten, but I remember what my parents did for me – they sat me down and logically explained things to

使他们忙于作业、高尔夫练习和旅行。但这并不意味着我们剥夺了他们交友和正常社交生活的权利，错失了好多成长的乐趣。相反的，我们认为他们比大多数的孩子都快乐。在学校，无论是老师还是学校的职工都非常喜欢他们，因为他们不仅成绩好，还很有礼貌；在我们高尔夫球俱乐部，会员们都很羡慕他们漂亮的挥杆，也很喜欢他们得体的行为举止，很乐意跟他们交往；在家里，我们基本很少责骂他们，也从不指挥他们干这干那，我们给予他们充分的自由去做他们想做的、高兴做的，因为他们很少会做那些我们不赞同的事情。

孩子们的反馈及评论：

玛诗：我当时太小了，实在不记得很久以前自己上学前班的第一天发生了什么事情，但是我很清楚地记得爸爸妈妈当时对我做过的事－－他们让我坐下，很清晰地给我分析了这件事，

me and talked to my teacher at school, asking her to pay a little more attention to my problem. Multiple times I have heard my father retell this story to people when their conversations involved discrimination. I do not know if their proactive actions actually changed anything in me and the way I look at the world now, but their attentions to our problems and their relentless efforts to solve them for us will be forever appreciated.

Garwin: You can understand why I was extremely unhappy when my parents pushed me to join SCJGA and to enter tournaments competing with many good junior golfers. Not only I had to get up at 4 o'clock in the morning and took a long drive (always I went back to sleep in the car) to tournaments, but also had to endure the humiliation of defeat at the end. The feeling of getting beaten and suddenly became an underdog was miserable and forced me to try harder to succeed. Looking back I think it was the right dose of medicine for me; it taught me a good lesson: no matter how good I am, there is always someone better. I have to learn to accept it as

然后又找到我的老师，拜托她多关注一下我。我听过很多次爸爸将我的故事讲给那些讨论种族歧视的朋友听。我不知道是不是爸爸妈妈这种积极主动的行为改变了我、以及我看世界的方式，但是他们对我们的关注以及不懈地为我们解决一个又一个的难题是使我终生难忘的。

家荣：当爸爸妈妈使我参加南加州青少年高尔夫球协会去和很多优秀的高尔夫球选手比赛的时候，我非常不高兴，因为我不仅要早上 4 点钟起床，还要坐很久的车去参加比赛（经常在车上睡着了），而且还要承受最终被打败的耻辱。这种突然成为失败者的的感觉简直让人难以忍受！但是现在回过头来看，这个决定对当时的我显然是苦口的良药，它使我明白，无论自己多么优秀，都会有人比自己更好，我必须学会接受，然后尽自己最大的努力做得更好，永不自满。

a life reality, and all I can do is to try my best while never being complacent.

Develop good character

Everybody knows that setting a *good example* is the single most important thing in child-rearing, for children tends to copy their parents. What is a better way to teach our children than by showing them ourselves? But it is easier said than done. We all have flaws and bad habits and we, ourselves, have to get rid of those bad examples first. We should not break our own rules and bring outside stresses home, we must show strength during difficult times and treat people with respect, and be a good citizen in front of our children. It is better showing no example (if we cannot be a good one) than *bad* example. Nothing is worse than showing our children what a bad person we are; we not only will lose our self-respect and credibility but also might lead them to follow our footsteps. But, many parents do just that; they dodge creditors by having their children lie for them, saying they are not home, they

发展优秀的品格

　　大家都知道，树立良好的榜样在养育孩子的过程中是一个至关重要的环节，因为孩子们很喜欢去模仿他们的父母，所以还有比我们亲自示范更好的方法么？但是这件事说起来容易做起来难。我们每个人都有自己的缺点和坏习惯，那么我们自己首先要去除这些坏榜样，例如我们要有原则，不要把外面的压力带回家里。应该展现给孩子们在逆境中的坚强、尊敬他人和做一个好公民的形象等等。如果不能成为孩子的好榜样，那没有榜样总比坏榜样强。没有什么比展示给孩子看我们是多坏的一个人更糟糕的事情了。这样我们不仅失了自重和信用，更会错误地引导孩子误入与我们相同的歧途。但是，好多家长们都如此行为：他们教孩子说谎来搪塞那些讨债的人，说他们不在家；

brag about their cleverness of buying something and then return it for full refund after having used it, and they make no effort to conceal those inappropriate behaviors – flirting, cheating, stealing, fighting, smoking and getting drunk. Even their bad eating habits have negative effects on their children; obese parents are most likely having obese children.

However, just setting good example is not enough, we must have the right methods to teach. We have seen so many bad children with good parents or just the opposite. I have a schoolmate whose father was a janitor, but he was a very good student and eventually became a medical doctor. So many times when I went over to his apartment, I heard his father scold him, "You lazy boy, you want to make a living with a *broom* like me?" And sometimes I heard his mother say to him, "Don't waste money like that. Can't you see how hard your father work to support us?"

In our case, we not only try to set good examples but seize *every* opportunity – during

或者吹嘘他们很聪明，因为刚刚把用过的商品又退回给商家；他们也从没试图将自己那些不合适的行为习惯隐藏起来，譬如，调情、欺骗、偷窃、打架、吸烟、酗酒等等；就是不好的饮食习惯都会对孩子们有很负面的影响，超肥胖的家长很可能有肥胖的孩子。

不过，仅仅树立好的榜样是不够的，我们必须还要有正确的教育方法。我们碰到过好多坏孩子却有好的父母，亦或者相反的情况。我有一个同学，他的爸爸是个清洁工人，但是他是一个很好的学生，后来成为了一名医生。很多次我去他家，都听到他的爸爸说："你这个懒孩子，难道你想像我一样靠扫帚维持生计吗？"。有时候也会听到他妈妈对他说："不要那样浪费钱，你没看到你爸爸是多么辛苦地工作赚钱养家么？"

就我们自己而言，我们不仅树立了好的榜样，并且抓住了每个机会——在吃饭的时候、

dinners, in the car going places or taking a leisurely walk together – to stimulate our children's correct thinking. My wife and I would talk about social issues and family affairs intended for our children to hear. They might not have any response at the time but they had *heard* us. For many years later they would say something we had said before or have opinions similar to ours. Somehow, they had been greatly influenced by our conversations without participation.

Realizing the world is getting smaller due to the great improvement of worldwide transportation and more complex because of the melting-pot effect of multi-cultures, I see the need to prepare our children for a different world, a much more dangerous world where cheaters, scoundrels, swindlers, and all sorts of criminals abound. They are born in America where honor and honesty are the norms and to be treasured. They are too trusting and tend to be easy victims for criminals. In order to protect themselves, they must know all these criminal activities, not to

在去某地的车上、在散步的时候——来激发孩子们正确的思考。我和太太经常讨论一些有关社会和家庭的话题特意让孩子们听。开始的时候他们可能没有任何反馈，不过他们在听！这样过了很多年之后，他们会说出我们之前说过的话，或者有与我们相似的观点。所以即使没有参与其中但他们还是被我们的谈话深深的影响了。

由于交通工具的不断发展和各民族间的不断融合，我们的世界变得越来越小，同时犯罪率也在不断升高，所以我意识到我们的孩子需要为这些做好准备。他们出生在崇尚荣誉和诚信并以此为做人准则的美国。他们太容易相信他人，因此很容易上当受骗。为了能保护自己，他们必须了解这些犯罪行为，这并不是为了将这些用在他人身上，只是希望他们可以识别犯罪行为，并知道如何处理它。

use them to prey on other people, but to detect criminals and know how to deal with them.

But, I have to admit that my way of teaching, though very effective, was a little extreme and unconventional and, for sure, often misunderstood and disapproved by most honest and straight-forwarded people like our children. When they were little kids, I would encourage them to steal a candy or a fruit from the market by doing it myself. They were horrified and ran away as fast and as far away from me as they possibly could, lest they would be caught together with me. Since they had demonstrated to me that they knew stealing was wrong and they did not want to be a thief, I had no need to teach them the other half – the wrong and the consequence of stealing. The same with cheating; I knew they were not cheaters when they disapproved my cheating them on golf and card games. But trying to convince them it is necessary sometimes to lie was difficult; to them a lie is a lie and they could not believe there is such a thing as a "good" lie.

Are We Lucky or What

虽然我的方法很有效，但是我不得不承认，这种教育方法很极端、很不合规矩，对于我们孩子这种诚实、正直的这类人来说，很难被赞同。他们小的时候，我怂恿他们从超市里偷一块糖或者一个水果，他们怕的要命，不敢去偷。我偷时他们便撒腿就跑，跑的远远的、离我远远的，生怕我们被一起抓到。因为他们的行动已经告诉了我，偷窃是不对的，他们不想成为小偷，那么我就不需要教他们剩下来的那部分——偷窃是错误的，以及偷窃的后果是什么了。对于欺骗的行为，我的方法是一样的。在我们打高尔夫和玩纸牌的时候，我经常要一些小手段来欺骗他们，他们很不赞同我这种做法，所以我又知道了，他们是不会想成为骗子的。但是，我却很难使他们相信，有时候谎言是必须的，因为对于他们来讲，谎言就是谎言，根本不存在什么"善意的谎言"。

That was the reason we made them – forced them to be more accurate – to spend a few summers living in Hong Kong when they were young, to learn to be street smart in one of the most complicated places in the world. Just after two summers, we could notice the huge difference. Now, they both work and live in Hong Kong and fit in comfortably, which we do not think possible if they have not been spending some time there. But, their minds are still too pure; they see only the good things in a person. I still remember that my son said I have an *evil* mind when I tried to predict some bad things out of a person. But, I hope someday after he has seen enough bad people, he will instead know his father has a *good* mind.

But, we think the biggest help was the introduction of golf to them. Many people asked us why in the world we chose *golf* for our children when it was conceived as an old man's game in the Eighties and before Tiger Woods helped making it popular. They admired our vision of seeing golf's coming of

Are We Lucky or What

　　他们小的时候,我们要(強迫比較適当)他们在香港待了几个夏天,希望他们会在这个世界上其中一个最复杂的地方慢慢拥有更好的应变能力,迫使他们更加准确地判断对与错。结果,仅仅在那里待了两个夏天,我们就发现了他们的巨大变化。现在他们两个都在香港工作生活,我们觉得如果没有之前那段时间的学习,他们不会像今天一样适应那里的生活的。但是他们的思想还是太单纯,只看到人好的一面。我还记得我们儿子说我的头脑太邪恶,总是把人往坏的方面去想。但是我希望终有一天,在他见到了足够多的坏人之后,会认为他爸爸的头脑是灵活的。

　　但是,最大的帮助还是让他们接触了高尔夫球。很多人都问我们,为什么会给孩子们选择高尔夫球这项运动,因为八十年代那时,高尔夫被认为是老年人的运动,直到后来老虎·伍兹才使它流行起来。他们非常佩服我们的高瞻远瞩,

age. But they were wrong. We had no idea golf was going to be this popular then. The reasons for our choice were:

(I) We like golf and we play golf. It is one of the best games ever invented and it is an all-around game that requires both physical and mental abilities. It is a game you can play all your life with little chance of injury and by yourself or with others. Besides, what else is better than playing a game and doing exercise at the same time in a park-like environment?

(II) Most golfers are gentlemen and ladies; at least they act like one while they are playing golf. They are not necessary nice people but they generally are nice and polite to one another. We want our children to grow up in such environment.

(III) Golf is the only game that is self-policing. It is played by the rules and honesty and discipline are the important parts of the game. We believe golf can do a *better* job than we can to teach our children those good qualities.

但是他们错了，我们根本没有想到高尔夫会流行起来。当时选择它是因为我们有以下几点考量：

（一） 我们喜欢高尔夫，也打高尔夫。我觉得他是世界上最好的运动之一，这个运动不仅需要体力，还需要一定的脑力，而且运动的寿命可以长达一生，却很少有机会受伤。并且每个高尔夫球场都如公园一般，还有哪项运动的环境好过它的呢？

（二） 绝大多数打高尔夫球的都是绅士或者淑女，至少在打球的时候，他们会表现得如此。他们自己可能不是很随和，但是他们必须对其他人随和并且彬彬有礼。我们希望我们的孩子在这样的环境中长大。

（三） 高尔夫是唯一一项需要自律的运动。规则、诚信是这项运动的重要组成部分。在教育孩子拥有这样的品质上，我认为高尔夫比我们做的要好得多。

(IV) Like military training, golf requires discipline, hard work, mental and physical toughness, endurance, and perseverance. In tournament junior golfers must carry their own bags and walk the golf course. All these require tremendous physical and mental toughness.

(V) We were told by many college advisors, for our children going to top universities the chance is better if they have either special talents or are good at one of the major sports. Being Asians they are not built strong and tall and, therefore, they have disadvantages in most of the sports. Only in golf they have no such disadvantages because physical strength is not as important as mental strength.

Feedbacks and Comments:

Marcie: I do find myself greatly influenced by my parents' conversations that I'm exposed to; a lot of things did not make any sense to

（四） 就如同军人训练一样，高尔夫同样要求选手们有纪律性、不断努力、在精神和身体上有强大的意志力、耐受力以及坚持不懈的精神。在比赛中，选手们必须背着球包在球场上徒步走。這些都需要体力和毅力。

（五） 很多大学的顾问建议我们，如果孩子有某些特殊的天赋或者擅长某项体育活动，那么他们进入名校的机会就会更大一些。身为亚洲人他们的身材并不高，身量并不壮，所以在很多体育项目上都有很大的弱势，只有高尔夫这项运动对身材的要求没那么高，反而对精神层面要求更加多些。

孩子们的反馈和评价：

玛诗：我发觉经常听爸爸妈妈聊的那些话对我有很大的影响，原来小的时候真的不觉得，但是现在看来确实如此。

me at the time as they do now. I did not like golf at first when my father introduced me to it. It required many hours of practice, and it gave me callused hands and ugly face sunspots, yet I played it to better my chances of going to an elite university. I must admit it has been extremely relevant and applicable to other aspects of my life (for example, discipline, time management, handling stress and pressure). Also, golf has opened up many opportunities for me, in school and in the real world.

Garwin: I'm sure there are many ways to instill good moral character in a child, but I agree with my dad's sentiments. Being a good example and role model for a child is probably the most important, and I will try to do my best in this regard with my own family. Also, golf remains a big part of my life even though I rarely have time to play these days. Growing up playing the game competitively definitely helped me build character, and I do believe it had a hand in shaping who I am; I

爸爸刚开始让我学习高尔夫的时候我并不喜欢它，因为每天我要花好几个钟头练球，手上都磨出了茧子，脸上都晒出了斑点，但是我又不得不练习，因为它可以使我有更大的机会升入著名大学。同时我也得承认高尔夫也对我人生的其他方面有极大的影响（譬如自律性、时间的管理、处理压力的能力等等），它也带给我很多机会，无论是在学校还是在现实的生活中。

家荣：有很多方法可以灌输给孩一个有道德的人格，但我还是同意爸爸的观点，父母成为孩子们的好榜样和心中的偶像是很重要的，我会为了我的家庭努力做到这一点。虽然现在很少有时间打高尔夫，但是它在我的生命中还是占有很重要的地位的。从小到大参加了无数场的比赛，这对塑造我的性格有很大的帮助；

have learned a lot from the game itself and from the people whom I make contact through golf. And because my father is an avid golfer, we have a lot of fun playing golf together. Somehow, he is a completely different person when he plays golf; he jokes, laughs and even wagers with us. Oh, he always tries to cheat us, too! Perhaps, it is his way of teaching us honesty.

Are We Lucky or What

球赛本身和打球时所接触到的人，也使我从中学习到了很多。因为爸爸是一位狂热的高尔夫爱好者，所以我们一起打球的时候很开心。爸爸打球的时候仿佛就是另一个人，他爱说爱笑，还会开玩笑，甚至还和我们打赌。对了，还经常骗我们！可能，这是他教我们要诚实的方法吧。

Our ambitious plan

Our original plan was to make our two children professional golfers because, in our opinion, it is the best profession in the world; making a good living while playing golf. But we also realized the chance of success is very slim; a few succeed but many more fail. A lot of aspiring golfers end up working at pro shops for minimum wages or even worse, depressed and hopeless. Being responsible parents we do not want this to happen to our children. We must give them a *safety net*; in case they do not make it to our lofty goal, they will have something to fall back on. And that is a college degree from a prestigious university.

Our immediate goal was to get our children into elite colleges and play college golf, so that they would have four years of opportunity to prove if they were good enough to turn pro. If they were not, they

我们雄心勃勃的计划

我和太太开始的计划是让我们的孩子成为职业高尔夫球选手，因为在我们看来这是世界上最好的工作，既能打球还能赚钱。但是慢慢地我们觉得这个计划成功的机会很渺茫，在这条道路上只有那么几个人功成名就，绝大多数都是以失败告终。很多当时富有激情的选手最终沦落到去高尔夫球商店工作，赚着微薄的薪水，有的甚至感到失落跟绝望。作为负责任的父母，我们不希望这样的事情发生在我们的孩子身上。我们必须给他们准备个"备胎"，万一他们没有实现我们的宏伟计划，至少他们还可以有第二种选择。这个"备胎"就是一张著名大学的文凭。

所以当时我们的短期内目标是让我们的孩子能去名校念大学并在学校的高尔夫球队继续打球，这样他们就又多了 4 年的时间来验证自己是否能成为一名职业高尔夫球选手。如果不是，

would at least have a very valuable diploma to get a good job. Once we had a plan, we worked diligently toward our goal step by step. We hired golf coaches, enrolled them into junior golf associations, joined private golf club, into high school golf team, and entered tournaments, a lot of tournaments, especially the American Junior Association's tournaments where coaches from major universities came to hunt for good players. We both accompanied them to tournaments all over the country during the summer, and for the rest of the year, we were playing golf with them in the afternoon, after school and before dinner. Not only had we spent a small fortune on them but also a lot of our time. But we did not regret. It was a very rewarding experience and a privilege to *watch* our children grow, in the right direction and into a bright future.

Many of you may wonder if golf really helped our children getting into Harvard. We believe it *did*. Why? Because Harvard has a very high academic requirement and because

那他们至少还有一个含金量很高的学历来获得一份好工作。既然已经定下了计划，那接下来我们便朝着这个目标一步步地不断前进，我们给孩子们请了私人教练、让他们参加了青少年高尔夫球协会、私人高尔夫球俱乐部、高中的高尔夫球队，还有很多锦标赛，尤其是全美青少年高尔夫球锦标赛，在那里，有很多来自各大学的高尔夫球教练为学校挑选优秀的选手。每年夏季，我和太太两人陪着他们走遍全美好多地方参加各种锦标赛。平时每天下午、放学后、晚饭前，便陪着他们练球。我们不仅在他们身上花了很多钱，同时也付出很多时间，但是我们从没后悔过。见证孩子们朝着正确的方向、光明前途成长是很有成就感的经历和值得庆幸的事情。

　　你们可能会问，高尔夫是不是真的对我的孩子进入哈佛有一定的帮助。我认为是这样的，的确如此。为什么呢？哈佛对学生的文化课要求很高，因为他的声誉吸引了很多有才华的申请者，

its prestige it attracts many high caliber applicants, so many that each year it rejects more than 90% of its applicants, including many valedictorians. But to recruit good golfers for their golf team, who meet its high academic requirement is difficult, for golf requires a lot of time to practice and play that most good golfers are bad students and good students are bad golfers. Our children happened to be good at both, school and golf. Playing in the AJA's golf tournaments had also helped; it gave our children the opportunities to meet and befriend with university coaches, which we believe had helped a great deal in their admissions.

Why Harvard, you may ask, of all the great universities in the world? The reasons are quite obvious: Harvard is the oldest major university in the country, has the second largest library (behind Library of U.S. Congress) and is the second richest organization in the world, after Vatican. With that kind of money, power and prestige, it

太多了所以每年都要拒绝好多优秀的高中毕业生。但是在招收优秀的高尔夫球选手上，同时要求他们有很好的学业成绩却是十分困难的，因为这些选手们需要很多时间来练习、打比赛，所以好多高尔夫打的好的文化课成绩都不好、成绩好的球打得不好，而我们的孩子呢，恰好两方面都很出色。还有，参加全美锦标赛，它使我们的孩子有机会与这些大学教练结识，对他们入学也起了很大的作用。

那再说一说，为什么要去哈佛呢？你可能会问"世界上这么多著名的大学，为什么你们会选择哈佛？"答案显而易见：哈佛是美国历史最悠久的大学，它还拥有全世界第二大的图书馆，仅次于美国国会图书馆；它也是全世界第二富有的组织，第一名是梵蒂冈的罗马教廷。有了钱、权和名誉，

attracts the best faculties and the brightest students. Moreover, there are many other hidden benefits going to Harvard, such as: the accessibility to its vast network of alumni, state-of-the-art facilities, and to the pool of talents and other resources. Just its name alone is able to open many doors. Yes, we want our children to have the best and all these are the reasons that we had chosen Harvard for them.

Feedbacks and Comments:

Marcie: I am glad that our parents *did give* my brother and me a safety net, which is a good education to fall back on in the event that we could not make it to become professional golfers. Now, even though we did not fulfil our parents' dream, we at least had a good education, which taught me to think and write critically, meet the right kind of people, and have access to opportunities that otherwise would not have been accessible were it not for Harvard.

它会拥有最好的院系、吸引最优秀的学生。甚至还有一些潜在的优势，例如，很强大的校友关系网、最先进的设施、设备、天才们的圈子和一些其他的资源等等。仅仅"哈佛"这个名字就可以敲开好多扇门。我希望孩子们能得到最好的，这就是我们为什么会让他们选择哈佛的原因。

孩子们的反馈和评价：

玛诗：我非常庆幸爸爸妈妈给我和弟弟选择了一个"备胎"，如果我和弟弟没有办法成为职业高尔夫球选手，那我们最起码还有一个出色的教育背景可以依靠。虽然我们没能实现爸爸妈妈的宏伟计划，但是我们至少接受了良好的教育，并学会了如何客观地思考和表达，有机会去接触一些合适的人、拥有除了哈佛其他学校不能给予的更多的机会。

Garwin: I am glad too, glad that they are practical dreamers. While I believe myself to be a decently intelligent person, I grew up with a lot of kids who I thought were equally smart and capable. Yet, for whatever reason, few applied themselves to the extent my sister and I did, and even fewer ever considered applying for a school like Harvard. Perhaps one reason is because no one ever told them to set that as a goal. In many quantifiable ways, the chances of getting into Harvard are actually much higher than say, making a living in the NBA (National Basketball Association). Yet, I would wager that most kids on a playground would see themselves as the next Michael Jordan before they see themselves playing ball for Harvard. I have no idea what my life would be like if I had not gone to a very good college, but I do see the benefits it has brought me. Getting there required a work ethic and self-discipline that is now a natural part of me and it has also given me the self-confidence that I am capable of tackling new challenges.

家荣：我和姐姐一樣也很庆幸，爸爸妈妈是很实际的梦想家。我自认为是个比較聪明的人，当然，周围和我一起长大的很多孩子也很聪明、很有能力。可是因为各种各样的原因，他们很少有能做到我和姐姐这样的，更少有像我们考入哈佛这样的名校的。可能其中的一个关键的原因就是没有人告诉他们要把这些作为他们的目标。从某种程度上讲，考入哈佛大学的机会要比进入 NBA 打球成为一个職業籃球选手的机会高得多。但是我敢打赌，操场上多数的孩子都会梦想自己成为下一个迈克尔·乔丹而不是为哈佛大学打球。我真的不敢想象如果没有进入一所好大学读书，我的命运将会变得怎样，但是我却真实地体会了它带给我的诸多益处。进入哈佛需要勤奋和自我约束能力，现在他们已经成为了我的一部分，同时哈佛也给予了我自信，使我相信我有能力接受各种各样新的挑战。

Success

After four years of playing college golf, it proved our children are not professional golfer materials. Harvard is not famous for golf; it is famous for academic achievements. Although they did not fulfil our high expectations, they have not disappointed us, either. We consider their accomplishments more than satisfactory and we are very proud of them. We do not want to brag about their financial success and that is not what this book is about. We want to focus on their personal success which we think is far more important than the financial one, for financial success does not necessarily require hard work, discipline and constant self-improvement. Any person with an ambition, luck or a ruthless mentality might be able to achieve it. That is why we do not call drug dealers, swindlers, kidnappers and robbers successful people. We despise them even they have money. Nor do we consider rich heirs

成功

在四年的大学高尔夫生涯结束后，事实证明他们不适合成为职业高尔夫球选手。哈佛以学术成就著名，而高尔夫并不是它的强项。虽然孩子们没有实现我们的高期望，但是他们也没有让我们失望。他们的成就已经使我们很满意了，我们为他们而感到自豪。在这里我不想过多地赘述他们在金钱上的成就，因为这不是我这本书的重点，我反而更加关注他们的个人品行的成就，这与金钱比起来要重要的多。因为金钱上的成就有时候并不需要勤奋努力、自我约束或者不断的自我提高，任何一个对金钱有着极度的热情、有运气或者冷酷无情的人都有可能成为富翁，这就是为什么我们不认为那些毒贩、诈骗犯、绑架的匪徒、抢劫犯是成功的人，即使他们很有钱我们也看不起他们；还有那些富家子或者彩票大赢家，可能我们会羡慕他们的运气，但我们也并不认为他们是成功的人。

and lottery winners successful people, though we might envy their lucks.

What we consider a successful person has nothing to do with money or position or status. All these fat bank accounts, fancy cars, big houses and fame do not make a person successful. A successful person is kind, respectful and helpful to others, a law-abiding citizen who plays by the rules, pays taxes, contributes to the societies and, most importantly, who is happy and a good example for his/her family. We are proud to say that our children have accomplished all these, and they have not disappointed us for all our efforts to raise them.

Many friends think our children's success is the result of their own intelligence. They would say, "They're very smart." But they are wrong! Our children were not born smarter; their natural intelligence is about average, no better and no worse than those of average children. If they are smarter, it is because they have acquired it after birth rather than born with. Since the time when they

我们认定的成功人士与金钱、地位、名誉都没有任何关系。那些巨额的银行存款、名车、豪宅、名誉并不能使一个人成功。一个成功的人应该是友好的、受人尊敬的，经常帮助他人的人，他遵纪守法、照章纳税对社会做出贡献，更重要的是，他是一个乐观积极向上的人、同时也是家人的好榜样。我们可以非常自豪地说，我们的孩子就是这样的人，他们并没有让我们失望，没有辜负我们对他们的一番教导。

很多朋友认为我们孩子的成功是源于他们的高智商，并且总是说："他们很聪明。"但是我认为这种说法是错误的。我们的孩子不是与生俱来的聪明，他们的智商与其他正常孩子无异。如果说他们更聪明些，那是因为后天的习得而不是天生如此。

were babies and continued to adulthood, I always fooled them, challenged them, and tried to catch their foolish mistakes to embarrass them. We still have videos that show I had spent hours at a time to test them with all kinds of questions, from arithmetic to spelling and from social science to natural science. But most important of all, I taught them *common sense.*

I still remember I always asked them questions (questions that are appropriate for their age) in the car when I took them to school. If they answered correctly, they would hear "good, smart!" from me and if their answers were wrong, they would hear "stupid!" instead. Many parents probably do not agree with my calling our children "smart" or "stupid", but we think it is important to let them know, all the time, what they are, *smart* or *stupid*. Knowing is a catalyst for wanting to learn and to improve. Only stupid people do not know they are stupid.

从他们是婴儿的时候开始到他们长大成年，我经常愚弄他们，挑战他们，抓住他们那些愚蠢的错误使他们难堪。我现在还保存有一些视频，记录了我当时每次都会花几个小时考查他们各种各样的问题，从算术到单词拼写、从社会科学到自然科学，但是最重要的是我还会教她们一些基本常识。

我还记得我经常在送他们上学的路上问他们问题（当然都是适合他们年龄的问题）。如果他们回答对了，我就会说："好，很聪明！"；如果回答错误，我就会说："真笨！"很多家长可能不会赞同我说他们"聪明"和"笨"，但是我认为，时刻让他们知道自己是聪明还是愚蠢是很重要的。了解自己就仿佛催化剂一般使他们更加有欲望去学习和提高。只有笨人才不知道自己是愚蠢的。

Feedbacks and Comments:

Marcie: I am very grateful for my parents. They did all the right things that good parents should do for their children. I am who I am due to a combination of my natural abilities and personality as well as my parents' guidance, unlimited love, patient nurture, and unselfish sacrifice; this is just one way of raising kids.

Garwin: I totally agree with my sister on this, but there is another very important aspect I want to mention, and that is: our parents never compared us with other people; they always think it is irrelevant because every person is different – different level of intelligence and ability, family background and opportunity. They are always very supportive but they demand us to do our best. Also, they are not like most Asian parents who push their children into lucrative professions, such as doctors and lawyers, without considering their children's interest,

孩子们的反馈和评论：

玛诗：我非常感激我的父母，他们做了所有称职的父母应该为孩子做的事情。在他们耐心的引导和培养下、无私的奉献和无尽的爱的陪伴下，我的个人能力和品格都得到了很好的发展。这是培育孩子其中之一的方法。

家荣：在这一点上，我非常同意姐姐的话。还有另外一个很重要的方面，那就是我们的爸爸妈妈从来没有拿我们和别人比较，他们认为那样是不公平的，因为每个人都是不同的，他们有不同的智商、不同的能力、不同的家庭背景、不同的机遇等等。他们很支持我们，但是要求我们自己要尽最大的努力。同时，他们也不像很多亚裔的父母亲一样不考虑孩子们的兴趣，强迫他们的孩子去学一些很热门的专业，譬如，医生、律师；

and try hard to influence them to marry into rich families with total disregard of their children's future happiness. Our parents never did any of these to us. They let us make our own choice; either it is our friends, our careers or our marriages. We have absolute freedom to do what we think is right for us, and for that I am forever grateful.

或者不考虑孩子将来的是否快乐，硬要他们和富有的人家结婚。我们的父母从没有那样做过，无论是交友、职业还是婚姻，他们都由我们自己來选择。我们有绝对的自由去做我们认为是对的事情，因此我也会永遠感激他们。

Our Mistakes

It is inevitable that we have made some mistakes in raising our children, for it is a very difficult task for any parent. It not only covers a long span of time, but also involves our children who are liable to be *affected* by not only us but also their peers, teachers, and the society they live in. Furthermore, it is difficult to determine what we have done is right or wrong. We just do not have the chance to do it all over again and try out different approaches. At the end we have a lot of "*Ifs*" remained with us. The following are some of them:

I am a funny person with friends but somehow I cannot be funny with my family, especially with our children. I put on a different face, a very serious face. Even playing a game of golf or a card game with them, I was very critical of their mistakes and embarrassed them by treating them as though they were stupid people. What *if* I had more

我们的错误

我们在养育孩子的过程中，不可避免的会犯一些错误，因为这对任何一位家长来说都不是一件容易的事儿。它不仅持续的时间很长，而且我们的孩子还参与其中，他们不仅仅受我们父母的影响，周围的同龄人、老师、社会都在无时无刻地影响着他们。还有就是我们很难来断定我们的所作所为是对还是错。我们没有第二次机会重新再来尝试另一种完全不同的方法。所以最终留给我们的是好多，好多的"如果"，以下就是其中的一些：

我和朋友在一起的时候是个很风趣的人，可是我却对家人风趣不起来，尤其是对孩子们。面对他们的时候我总是换上另一副面孔，非常严肃的面孔。甚至是平时打高尔夫或者玩牌的时候，我对他们犯的错误也总是很苛刻，使得他们很难堪，就好像他们是很蠢的人一样。如果跟他们能多一些风趣少一些严肃，那他们会不会就没那么怕我，对我会更像对朋友一样？

fun with them and less seriousness, would they be less afraid of me?

Also, I am a dominating and very opinionated person; I voice my opinions too often, too honestly and very inconsiderately. I cut off and corrected my wife, undermining her authority with our children so many times that I wonder our children would be more affectionate to me *if* I had not done so.

There are many more unanswerable "*ifs*" mistakes I have made that I am not sure of, but there is one I am absolutely sure of; I acted the "bad guy" role too well – I am the bad guy and my wife the good guy. I was too stern and tough that our children were *afraid* of me. We were together a lot of time but we were *never* close. I never hugged them and they never did that to me, just like my father was with me. Now that they are adults and I am sure they love me and respect me, but we have difficulty showing affection to each other. So often I envy my wife and wonder why I was so stupid not to choose to act the

　　还有，我是一个操纵欲很强并且很主观的人，经常把自己的想法坦露无遗，根本不考虑别人的感受。很多次，在孩子面前我打断或者纠正太太的观点，破坏了她在孩子们心中权威的形象，有时候我就在想，如果我不这么做，孩子们是不是会对我更亲近些。

　　还有很多我无法回答的"如果"这类问题，但是有一件事情我是非常肯定的，我扮演"坏人"这个角色扮演得实在太好了（我扮演"坏人"，太太扮演"好人"），我太不苟言笑、太严厉了，所以孩子们都很怕我。我们待在一起的时间很多，但是我们的关系不是很亲密。我从没有拥抱过他们，他们也从没有这样对待过我，就像我的父亲对待我一样。现在他们长大成人了，我很肯定他们是爱我的、尊敬我的，但是给予对方亲密的举动对我们来说却是很难的事情。很多时候我甚至羡慕我的太太，猜想着我为什么这么傻不去选择当"好人"这个角色，让太太去当"坏人"呢。

"good guy" role and let my wife act the part of a "bad guy".

Feedbacks and Comments:

Marcie: Our father is a good person and a good parent; he really cares about us and provides well for us. But he is too stern and harsh to us, and he often hurts our feelings by treating us like an idiot with his criticism and teaching. He is a lucky guy though; he married our mother who is a wonderful person and mother, who always makes up for our father's shortcomings by saying, "Your father's always like this, but he loves you and cares for you."

Garwin: My sister and I are lucky to have a mother like ours, and without her I do not think we are the same persons as we are now. Anyway, our father is just too stern and unapproachable to be a good parent without a good wife like our mother to help him. But I

孩子们的反馈和评论：

玛诗：我们的爸爸是个好人，也是一位好父亲，他真的很关心我们，给我们提供最好的东西，但是他对我们太严厉太苛刻了，他的批评和教育方法让我们感觉自己就像个傻瓜一样，这真的使我们感情上很受伤害。但是，不得不说，他是一个很幸运的人，幸运地娶到了我们的妈妈。她是那么好的一个人，一个好妈妈，她经常帮爸爸弥补他的的不足，安慰我们说："你们的爸爸就是这样的，不过他是很爱你们，很关心你们的。"

家荣：姐姐和我都觉得有这样的妈妈真的是很幸运，没有妈妈，我们可能不会有今天的成就。爸爸如果没有妈妈的帮助，他那样严厉又难以接近的人也不会成为一个好家长。

am convinced he is very wise; he always has a lot of good ideas and has the amazing ability to get our mother to go along with him.

但是我承认，爸爸是个很聪明的人，他经常会有很多好主意，同时也很有本事让妈妈能跟着他的想法走。

Testimonials

Maybe we are lucky or maybe not, but for us it is important to know that we have helped our children to achieve the most that their potentials allow. We are sure there are a lot of children do better or worse than ours, depending upon a lot of other factors besides their own abilities. But as long as they live up to their potentials and become good and productive citizens, we should be proud to declare: "We're *good* parents." We are glad that our children are happy with the way they had turned out to be, and that is very important to us. We are not boastful people and we do not want to advertise it, but for the sake of proving it to you, our readers, that this book is worth your time to read, we are going to share with you a few of our Birthday, Mother and Father's Day cards from our children. We are confident that you, after having read them, will agree with us that we had not been wasting our time and money on them.

贺卡

可能我们很幸运，也可能不是，但是对于我们来说，最重要的是帮助孩子们发挥了他们最大的潜能。我们知道有很多孩子比他们做的还要好，也有很多不如他们，这除了他们个人的能力之外，还有很多其他因素的影响。不过，只要他们能依靠自己的能力成为一个好人、对社会有用的人，那么我们就可以自豪地说："我们是合格的父母。" 我们很高兴孩子们很满意他们现在的状态，这对我们来说也很重要。我们不是喜欢吹嘘的人，也不喜欢到处宣扬，但是为了证明给各位读者这是一本值得一看的书，我还是想和大家分享一下孩子们送给我们生日和各种纪念日的贺卡。我敢肯定，在你看完之后你一定会同意我们在孩子们身上花的时间和金钱都是值得的。

Dear Mommy, Happy Mother's Day!

You are truly my best role model on how to be a wonderful mom. Not only that, you also set a good example for me on how to be a caring friend, sister, and a supportive wife. Even though at times it may seem I do not learn from you, I have carefully watched how you lovingly treat other people (whether friends or family members) in the past 24 years. Your actions have taught me so much about being a strong, independent yet sensitive and thoughtful woman. You are truly a perfect human being – no one has all the combinations that you have (talented, beautiful, intelligent, funny, and most importantly, having a good heart).

You're the best, lovely Mommy!

Love you! Marcie – May 2003

贺卡 1

亲爱的妈咪：

你是我最好的榜样，教我如何成为一个伟大的妈妈。不仅如此，你还教会了我怎样成为一个贴心的朋友、姐姐和一名贤内助。在过去的 24 年中，虽然我好像没有真真正正地跟你学习，可是每次我都很认真地观察着你如何地关心朋友和家人。你的行动让我觉得自己也要成为像你一样坚强、独立、感情细腻、有思想的女性。你是如此优秀的人，没有人会有你那么多的优点－－很有才华、漂亮、聪明、风趣，最重要的是你有一颗善良的心。

您是世界上最好、最可爱的妈咪！祝您母亲节快乐！我爱您！

爱你的

玛诗　2003 年 5 月

Hi Mom, Happy Mother's Day!

It would have been a great honor just to know such a wonderful human being, but to have been able to be your son is the greatest gift I could ever ask for. I understand that this may be the happiest Mother's Day that I get to spend with you, but I want you to know that whatever the distance between us, I will always be thinking of you. Without your love and support through the years, I know I wouldn't have accomplished anything. You have always been the brightest star when I was in darkness and the truest compass when I needed direction. The seventeen roses represent the number of years you have been my mother. I chose white and yellow roses because they represent the kindest and gentlest colors; they represent you.

And do not be sad when the flowers eventually wither away, just like the years have gone by. There are bigger and happier years ahead, and I look forward to everyday I get to be the son of the Greatest Mom in the World!

Love always,

Garwin 2003

贺卡 2

妈妈：　祝您母亲节快乐！

能认识您这么好的人，已经是很幸运了，能生为您的孩子更是我有生以来最好的礼物。我知道这可能是我能陪您那么长时间一起庆祝的最后一个母亲节，但是我希望您知道，无论我们的距离有多遥远，我都会时时想念着您。这些年来如果没有您的爱与支持，我不会有任何成就。您是黑暗的夜空中最明亮的那颗星，更是我在迷失方向时给我指引方向的指南针。17 朵玫瑰代表了 17 年您对我的关怀与抚养，我选择了白色和黄色，因为它们代表着友善和温和，就如您一样。

即使日后这些花儿凋落了也请不要忧伤，它们就如同逝去的年华一样，即使已成过去，还会有更好更快乐的日子在前方等着我们。我期待着做您儿子的每一天，因为您是世上最好的妈妈！

永远爱你的

家荣　2003 年

Dear Daddy,

Even though you'll be spending Father's Day away from all of us this year, we'll still be thinking about you, like we do on any given day. Both Garwin and I carry out your life's guidance/advice in many aspects of our daily lives. Sometimes we don't even realize the impact you have on the choices we make until afterwards.

The time we've spent together as a family this year in HK has been invaluable. Even though we didn't do much together in terms of sight-seeing, it's the little things in everyday routine that we were all a part of that counts the most.

Happy Father's Day!   Love,

Marcie 2010

贺卡 3

亲爱的爸爸：

虽然今年您将度过一个没有我们陪伴的父亲节，但是身在远方的我们仍然会如以往一样想念您。日常生活的很多方面我和家荣都是遵照您的指导和建议去行事，很多时候连我们自己都没有意识到您对我们的影响是如此之大。

今年我们全家相聚在香港的时光是多么令人难忘。虽然我们只是到处转转并无其他，可这些日常的小事正因我们全家人的参与而变得珍贵无比！

祝您父亲节快乐！

爱您的　　　　玛诗 2010 年

Dad,   June 2010

Happy Father's Day!

It was nice to have you spend the last couple weeks with Marcie and me in Hong Kong. It is interesting that you and Mom had left Hong Kong so long ago, and yet now both Marcie and I are trying to make a life for ourselves in this part of the world.

I think it goes to show the support and wisdom you have given us has allowed us to explore new paths in life with confidence. For this, we will forever be grateful. Thank you, and have a Great Father's Day!

Love,

Garwin

贺卡 4

爸爸：

父亲节快乐！

很高兴过去的两个星期您和妈妈能来香港看我和玛诗。当年您和妈妈离开香港搬去美国，现在我和玛诗又回来这里工作生活，这是一件多么有趣的事情啊！在这样一个陌生的地方，正是因为您以往的教导以及给予我们的智慧，才能使我们如此自信地开辟新的人生道路。仅是这点，足使我永远地感激您，谢谢您，爸爸！再次祝您父亲节快乐！

爱您的

家荣　2010 年

Dear Dad: Happy Birthday!

I think this card is quite appropriate for you because you really are getting old. But, I think old age comes with its advantages: wisdom and respect from others around you. As I continue to mature and get older and hopefully wiser myself, I am realize more and more how fortunate I am to have had someone like you guiding me along the way. Your wisdom is inherent in what you have achieved and the foundation that you have established for Marcie and me, and hopefully we will continue to accomplish things in life that reflects that guidance and wisdom. Thank you for the years of patience and fatherly advice, and I look forward to much more to come!

Love, Garwin '09

贺卡 5

亲爱的爸爸：

　　　　生日快乐！

　　我觉得这张卡片很适合您，因为您真的变老了。不过我觉得年纪大了也有年纪大的好处：更加睿智、更受人尊敬。

　　随着自己不断长大、更加成熟、希望自己也能更加睿智，我越来越觉得有像您这样一个人一路引导着我是一件多么幸运的事。您的成就，还有您为玛诗和我创造的一切基础，足可以印证了您的智慧，希望在今后的人生道路上，有您的这些指导我们能取得更多的成就。

　　谢谢您这些年的耐心与作为父亲的建议，希望今后也能继续听到更多来自您的建议。

　　　　　　　　爱您的，家荣　　2009 年

Feedbacks and Comments:

Marcie and **Garwin:** All the things that we wrote on the cards were our true feelings at the time. We still have the same feelings, but more so!

孩子们的反馈和评论：

玛诗和家荣：所有写在贺卡上的话都是我们当时的真情流露。我们现在的感想仍然如此，只多不少！

Are all children born equal?

It depends who you ask. There is no consensus answer, although people have been debating on this issue for thousands of years. One School says: all children are born with "good" qualities, just like a piece of white paper, clean and spotless; only after birth that they acquire the "bad" qualities which corrupt the "good" ones that they have to begin with. Only we parents can maintain their original "good" qualities by teaching our children the goodness and not the badness. The other School says just the opposite: they are all born with "bad" qualities, full of flaws and only through good teachings that their "bad" qualities can be removed and replaced by "good" qualities; otherwise, they will become wicked people when they grow up.

I believe both Schools are "right" and "wrong", because I believe in genetics and every child has a different genetic makeups;

孩子生来就是平等的吗？

这个问题的答案取决于你问的是谁。虽然人们已经就这个问题争论了几千年了，但是我们仍然没有一致的答案。有一种说法：人性本善，就是人刚刚出生的时候就如一张干净没有污点的白纸，只是在出生后，我们后天习得一些好的或者坏的品质，就像一位好的艺术家可以将一张白纸变成一幅美丽的画，而坏的画家却可以将同样的一张白纸变成难看的东西。作为家长道理是一样的，我们可以使我们的孩子成为好人，也可以使他们成为罪犯。还有另外一种说法：人性本恶，人生来即充满了瑕疵和缺陷，只有通过好的教育，我们才能去除那些缺点成为一位好人，否则等长大后就会成为更加邪恶的人。

我觉得这两种说法都有对的地方和不对的地方。我是比较相信遗传学的，每个孩子都有不同的基因组成，

some are born healthy and some are sick, some have good nature and some have bad, and so on. The list of differences is endless. These differences are *born* with; inherit from our parents. However, through *after-birth* trainings and teachings we might, to a certain degree, change a child's personality. But by how much and in which direction (good or bad) depends not only on the percentage of "good" or "bad" that is born with, but also on the effectiveness of the after-birth trainings and teachings. Provide that the effectiveness of after-birth trainings and teachings is the same; theoretically, a child that is born with a high percentage of "good" will be more likely to become good and less likely to become bad. The opposite is true for a child born with higher percentage of "bad". But in reality, due to so many other elements that may affect a child, the result may not be that predictable.

Then, you may ask, "Why should we spend that much time, money, and energy on after-birth trainings and teachings if our efforts may not produce positive results, and

有的健康，有的体弱多病；有的脾气好，有的脾气不好，等等。这个列举起来就太多太多了，这些都是与生俱来的，遗传自父母的。但是出生后的教育以及训练，从某种程度上来说，是可以改变一个孩子的行为习惯的。但是能改变多少，以及什么方向（是好，还是坏），不仅取决于孩子们的先天条件，还要看后天的教育以及训练的效果如何。如果后天的教育、训练效果相同，孩子的先天条件越好，那么他（她）成才的可能性就越大，反之亦然。但是在现实生活中，有太多的因素影响着我们的孩子，所以结果就很难预测了。

那你可能会问："既然我们的努力并不一定会带来好的结果，那么我们为什么还要在孩子出生之后花费那么多的精力呢？

why don't we let our children develop on their own, naturally?" My answer to you is: we always want to fulfil our responsibilities as parents and do our best for our children because we love them. If they turn out to be good, we'll be very proud of them and of ourselves. If they turn out to be bad, at least we will not feel guilty that we have not done our job as a good parent should.

为什么不让孩子自由成长？我的回答是："我们爱我们的孩子，所以我们要尽最大的努力扮演好家长的角色，尽到做家长的责任。如果他们将来很成功，我们会为他们和自己感到骄傲；如果结果相反，那我们至少不会因为没有尽到作为家长的职责而自责。"

Be a wise parent

Although our children have not disappointed us so far, there is no guarantee that they will not in the future. Like everything else, people are subjected to change and our children are no exceptions, especially after marriage when spousal influence is much stronger than parental influence. Since their spouses were raised by different parents and under different environments, their values, personalities, behaviors, habits and thinking are more likely to be different. Unfortunately, there is nothing we can do about it. Our job as parents is over the day when our children are no longer children, and it should be that way. Let go of them, let them fly, let them explore the world by themselves, let them make their own decisions and mistakes and let them flourish or perish. Our job as parents is done regardless of how well we have performed it.

做一个明智的家长

虽然我们的孩子至今还没有让我们失望，但不保证他们今后不会。就像很多事情一样，人总是会变的，我们的孩子也不例外，尤其是在他们结婚之后，这时配偶的影响会多过父母。由于他们配偶的父母和成长环境不尽相同，他们的价值观、行为习惯、思考方式都有可能与我们的孩子不同。但是我们却什么都做不了，因为我们作为父母的工作已经在他们成人的那天结束了。我们也正该如此，要让他们自己闯荡，振翅高飞，通过自己的努力去探索这个世界，让他们自己做决定，容许他们犯错，让他们自己斩获成功，接受失败。无论父母的角色我们演绎的有多成功，我们始终是要退出他们的舞台的。

Never ever attempt to assist your children in rearing their children. It is their jobs and responsibilities, not yours. Do not rob them of their parental privilege which is one of the many joys and pains of having children. Also, from a selfish point of view, we have already devoted a lot of our time on them and should not spend more on the next generation. We should save some for ourselves and our spouses, and use it wisely to enjoy and do what we want to do before we leave this world. We only have one chance!

Most people may not agree with us, but we strongly believe that we should not leave a fortune for our children, even if we have it. We believe that teaching them to be good citizens and providing them a good education (based on their own abilities) are sufficient enough. Anything more than that may spoil them and make them lazy, lacking the motivation to work hard and try their best; it also may deprive them their senses of accomplishments. I remember my father once asked me how often we used our swimming

Are We Lucky or What

不要赏试去帮助你的孩子抚养下一代。这是他们的工作和责任，不是你的。不要抢夺他们作为父母的权利，因为这是一个痛并快乐的过程。如果从自私一点的角度来说，我们已经奉献出了很多的时间给我们的孩子，不应该再花一些在下一代了。我们要留出一些时间给我们自己和我们的另一半，在离开这个世界之前，我们要利用这些时间来做我们想做的事情，我们仅仅有这一次机会！

可是很多人可能不认同我们的观点，但是我们坚信，即使我们有也不应该留财产给孩子们。我们觉得教导他们如何成人长进，按照他们的能力给他们提供良好的教育已经足够了，多过这些就有可能会宠坏他们、使他们懒惰、缺乏足够的动机去努力工作、拼搏；更有可能剥夺了他们的成就感。记得有一次我的父亲问我多久用一次我们的游泳池。

pool. I told him not very often because we spent a lot of time playing golf, and the water was too cold in the winter. We used it mostly on weekends during the summer.

"What a waste!" he said. "Why you spent that much money on something you seldom use?"

"Was it your money that built it?" I asked. But as soon as I said it and saw my father, startled by my question, speechless and unpleasant, I felt terribly sorry for my disrespectfulness. It was true that he did not pay for its construction. I dared to ask him such a question not because I wanted to hurt his feeling but because I was very proud of my own accomplishment. If it was his money that built it, I would never have had the courage to say such a thing! And because of this incident, I realized how important it is to give our children the "right" to have that feeling – the feeling of *self-made* – which probably is one of the most enjoyable things a person can have. Leaving them a fortune will

我告诉他不是很常用，因为我们经常打高尔夫，再者冬天的时候水很凉，我们只是在夏季的周末用它。

"那太浪费了！"他说。"你为什么把钱花在不常用的东西上？"

"这是你的钱建的么？"我问。不过我刚说完这句话就因为自己的不敬感到很惭愧、很后悔，因为我发现父亲因为我的回答而感到很震惊，一时间说不出话来，也很不高兴。建造这个游泳池的确不是他的钱，这是事实，我敢这样问他是因为我为自己的成就感到很自豪。如果这个泳池是花他的钱建的，我绝不会有胆子说出这样的话來！正是因为这件事，我意识到赋予我们孩子这样的"权利"是多么的重要。这种"自创"的感觉可能是一个人可以拥有的最快乐的事情。

not only take away that "right" from them, but also cause the loss of their self-respect. People, including their own children, might say, "They have rich parents."

Remember: The parents' home is always the children's home, but the children's home *is not* the parents' home. Even though our children have not changed and still love us just like they always did before, their spouses and children may not have the same feelings for us. A brief visit is fine, but we need to be mindful that we do not overstay our welcome, and always remember that we are only guests. So, behave like one and keep our mouths quiet and our opinions to ourselves. Since us older people have the tendency to teach because we have been doing it to our children for decades, it is not easy to change the habit. We better learn to play dumb, deaf and blind, and act a little senile. Believe me; it will help us to avoid a lot of unnecessary troubles.

留给他们财产不仅可能会拿走他们这种"自创感权利",更有可能会夺走他们的自尊。别人,甚至他们自己的孩子都会说:"他们只是有个有钱的爸妈而已!"

请记住:父母的家永远是孩子的家,可是孩子的家却不是父母的。即使我们的孩子跟他们小时候没有任何改变,他们仍然像以往那样爱我们,可是他们的另一半和他们孩子可能就不会对我们有相同的情感。一个短时间的拜访是可以的,但是我们要注意的是,不要一厢情愿的认为我们是受欢迎的,然后久住不走,我们要时刻牢记,自己只是客人而已。所以也请以客人的身份来要求自己,闭上我们的嘴,我们的意见憋在自己的肚子里。人老了,便总是喜欢说教,因为我们已经说了几十年自己的孩子了,这个习惯太难改了;我们最好能装聋作哑,装瞎子,然后再让自己看起来真的老的不成样子了,这样会帮我们省去很多麻烦。

A word for those who are singles or childless couples: Do not envy us parents with children; you do not know how lucky you are! For sure, you may have missed some of the fun in having children, but you have also missed a lot of the pains that come with having them, too! In the end, we are all the same – just lonely, old people, except with one difference: you took the *short cut* and we took the *detour*.

Are We Lucky or What

对于那些现在仍然单身或者丁克的夫妇，请不要嫉妒我们。你们不知道你们有多么幸运！当然，你们没有经历过养育孩子的乐趣，但同时你们也没有经历过养孩子的痛苦！最终我们都是一样的－－孤独的老人，但唯有一点不同的是：你们走了捷径，而我们走了弯路而已。

About the author and coauthors

Author:

Andrew S. S. Chan, seventy years old and a retired businessman. I have a B.S. in finance from University of California – Long Beach and a M.S. from University of Illinois. I have already written and published two books, "*The Invisible Rings*" and "*At the Tea House*", both in English. And a few more books are forthcoming. I always like literature and have read a lot of books, both Chinese and English. And I enjoy writing, especially novels, with the intention to touch and inspire people.

Coauthors:

Soling Chan, my wife, has a B.A. in music from University of Southern California.

Marcie Chan, my daughter, has a B.A. in sociology from Harvard University.

作者和合著者

作者：

陈树燊，今年 70 岁，是一位退休商人。曾在加州大学长滩分校获经济学学士学位，伊利诺伊大学取得硕士学位。目前已经出版了两本英文版图书《無形介子》和《茶楼舌战》，现在正在筹备其他作品。我非常喜欢文学，中文、英文的书我都很喜欢读，也喜欢写作，尤其是小说，希望可以感动和激励读者。

合著者：

陈素玲，我太太，南加州大学音乐学士学位。

陈玛诗，我女儿，哈佛大学社会学学士学位。

Garwin Chan, my son, has a B.A. in economics from Harvard University and a M.B.A. from Harvard Business School.

Translator:

Chanzi Wang, has a B.A. in Engish literature from Northeast Normal University, China.

Are We Lucky or What

陈家荣，我儿子，哈佛大学经济学学士，哈佛大学商学院工商管理硕士。

翻译：

王婵子，中国东北师范大学，英语学士学位。

37978524R00124